asian
graphics now

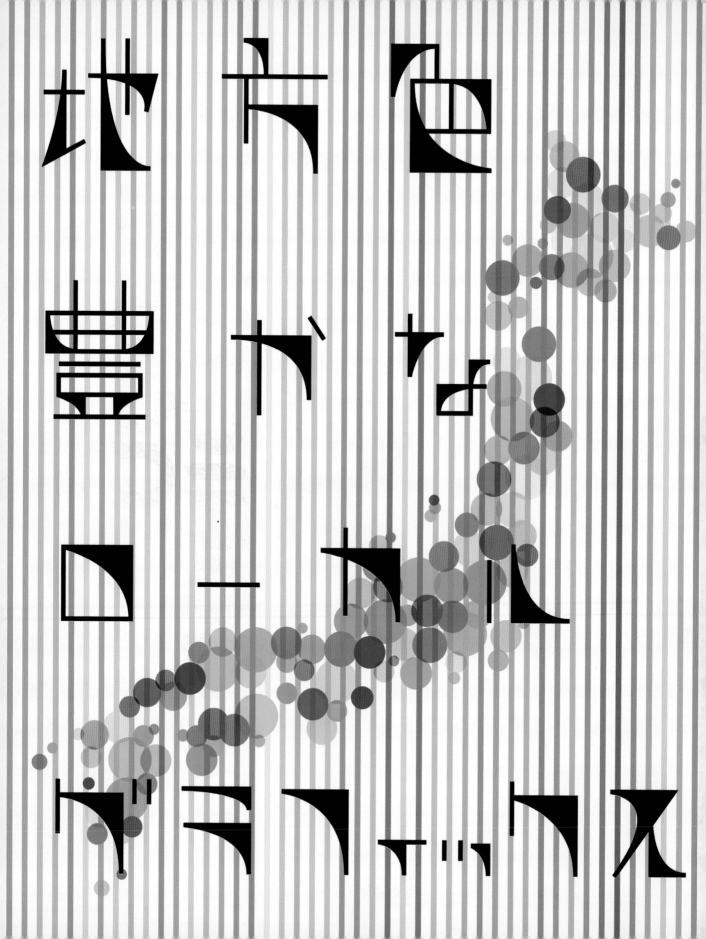

Ed. JULIUS WIEDEMANN

asian
graphics now!

TASCHEN

ESSAYS

CHaPTers

THE ASIAN MYSTERY

by Julius Wiedemann

I think it is fair to say that when it comes to Asia, it is the most diverse, and probably most mysterious continent in the world. Its 4 billion-plus inhabitants account for around 60 % of the world's population. It is officially composed of over 50 countries, according to the United Nations, spread over a territory where hundreds of languages and dialects are spoken. When it comes to graphic design then, it can be extremely hard to put all that into the same pot. People's idea of Asia can be very different too, as the continent is very often associated with China and Japan more than anything. These countries have polarised attention now for some years, with the first being a rising economic and political power, and the second being a mature and admired culture, as well as the second largest economy on the globe. Countries such as Indonesia, Thailand, Vietnam grab our attention more as great holiday destinations, while India, Taiwan, Singapore, Cambodia, and South Korea have their particular "brands", each one with its own individual characteristics.

So the challenge for the editing process is quite unique, and the objective was focused on showcasing how graphic design is developing in the region. This can give us an insight into how creativity operates

Wenn man von Asien spricht, erscheint es mir nur angemessen, von dem facettenreichsten und vermutlich geheimnisvollsten Kontinent der Erde zu sprechen. Seine über vier Milliarden Bewohner stellen etwa 60 % der Weltbevölkerung. Den Vereinten Nationen zufolge besteht Asien aus mehr als 50 Staaten, die sich über ein Territorium erstrecken, in dem Hunderte von Sprachen und Dialekte gesprochen werden. Es ist extrem schwierig, all das in Hinblick auf das Grafikdesign unter einen Hut zu bringen. Darüber hinaus verbinden die Menschen sehr unterschiedliche Vorstellungen mit Asien, da der Kontinent häufig vor allem mit China und Japan in Verbindung gebracht wird. Diese Länder polarisieren die Aufmerksamkeit nun schon seit mehreren Jahren: China aufgrund seiner wirtschaftlichen und politischen Macht, Japan aufgrund seiner ausgereiften und bewunderten Kultur und weil es die zweitgrößte Ökonomie der Welt ist. Länder wie Indonesien, Thailand oder Vietnam kennen wir eher als beliebte Urlaubsziele, während wir Indien, Taiwan, Singapur, Kambodscha und Südkorea als besondere „Marken" mit jeweils eigenen Charakteristika wahrnehmen.

Somit standen wir bei der Herausgabe dieses Buches vor einer einzigartigen Herausforderung mit dem vorrangigen Ziel, die

Il est à mon sens juste de dire que l'Asie est le continent le plus éclectique et certainement le plus mystérieux au monde. Avec plus de 4 milliards d'habitants, il représente environ 60 % de la population mondiale. Selon les Nations Unies, il compte officiellement plus de 50 pays répartis sur un territoire où des centaines de langues et de dialectes sont parlés. En termes de design graphique, il peut s'avérer très compliqué de placer tous ces ingrédients dans un même pot. L'idée que les gens se font de l'Asie peut aussi être très différente, sachant que le continent est souvent surtout associé à la Chine et au Japon. Depuis quelques années, ces pays attirent l'attention, le premier comme puissance économique et politique en pleine croissance, le second pour le fait d'être une culture mûre et admirée et la deuxième économie de la planète. Des pays comme l'Indonésie, la Thaïlande et le Vietnam attirent plus en tant que belles destinations touristiques, alors que l'Inde, Taiwan, Singapour, le Cambodge et la Corée du Sud affichent leur propre « marque » faite de caractéristiques individuelles.

Le défi pour l'élaboration de cet ouvrage est plutôt unique, l'objectif étant de montrer comment le design graphique se développe dans cette région. Il permet de se faire une idée de la créativité locale et pourquoi l'Asie

Future Academic
poster, 2008, by Allraid
Graphics, Japan

there, and why Asia fascinates so many of us. Its very dissimilar design industries make the selection of works especially harder. Japan might be said to be the only country with design in its veins, considered from a Western perspective, and that can be easily seen walking around Tokyo, or simply by looking at products from the acclaimed Muji brand. This is why the country accounts for a good part of the works featured here. Seoul, World Design Capital in 2010, is taking South Korea more into the spotlight, and the design industry is really reaching a bigger audience. Singapore also has very established associations with market and design, and its representation in the book really reflects that maturity. India is a very particular case, with its very distinguished visual culture, and a highly colourful, spiced-up Bollywood-type of graphic environment. It is probably the most far-out example of visual design in Asia. In China, on the other hand, graphic designers are commonly given shows in galleries, and their works walk between the lines of commercial and non-commercial, with a humorous and inspiring sense of experimentation.

In many countries it was difficult for us to communicate with and reach designers, so making contact with profess-

Entwicklung des Grafikdesigns in diesem Teil der Welt darzustellen. Dies kann Aufschluss darüber geben, wie Kreativität hier wirkt und warum Asien so viele von uns fasziniert. Die sehr unterschiedlichen Designbereiche des Kontinents erschwerten die Auswahl der Werke zusätzlich. Aus westlicher Sicht ist Japan das einzige Land, von dem man behaupten kann, dass ihm Design „im Blut" liegt. Das ist leicht nachzuvollziehen, wenn man durch Tokio schlendert oder sich einfach die Produkte der gefeierten Marke Muji anschaut. Darum stammt auch ein Großteil der hier vorgestellten Arbeiten aus diesem Land. Seoul, World Design Capital 2010, rückt Südkorea stärker ins Rampenlicht, und tatsächlich erreicht die Designindustrie hier ein wachsendes Publikum. Auch in Singapur sind Markt und Design schon lange stark miteinander verwoben. Dem wird durch eine entsprechende Gewichtung in diesem Buch Rechnung getragen. Indien ist mit seiner einzigartigen visuellen Kultur und einer höchst farbenprächtigen, von Bollywood angehauchten Grafiklandschaft ein Sonderfall: Hier finden sich wahrscheinlich die extremsten Beispiele für visuelles Design in Asien. In China hingegen stellen Grafikdesigner üblicherweise ihre Werke in Galerien aus. Geprägt von einem humorvollen und anregenden Gespür für Experimen-

fascine autant de personnes. Ses industries de design si dissemblables corsent la tâche de sélection des travaux. On peut dire que le Japon est le seul pays portant le design dans le sang d'un point de vue occidental, un design facilement appréciable dans les rues de Tokyo ou en observant les produits de la marque acclamée Muji. C'est pourquoi une bonne partie des travaux présentés dans ces pages proviennent de ce pays. Séoul, capitale mondiale du design en 2010, place la Corée du Sud en vedette, et le secteur du design touche un public accru. Singapour possède aussi des liens solides avec le marché et le design, et sa représentation dans l'ouvrage reflète parfaitement cette maturité. L'Inde est un cas très particulier, forte d'une culture visuelle très distinguée et d'un type d'environnement graphique relevé à la touche Bollywood. Il s'agit probablement de l'exemple de design visuel le plus d'avant-garde en Asie. En Chine, les designers graphiques bénéficient généralement d'expositions dans des galeries, et leurs œuvres passent du domaine commercial au non commercial avec un sens de l'expérimentation à la fois amusant et inspirant.

Dans de nombreux pays, il nous a été difficile de contacter les designers ; partie de notre tâche a donc souvent consisté à tenter

Untitled
poster, 2009, by Hoseob
Yoon, South Korea

***New Typographics with
Font Samples***
book design, 2005,
by Hajime Kabutoya,
Happy & Happy, Japan,
Pie Books

ionals and advisers in many places was a
key part of the job. We relied on many
of the most talented professionals and
design scholars in many of the countries,
to try to reach out as far as we could. The
result is a stimulating blend of cultures,
translated into great posters, book and
magazine design, logos, brochures, branding projects, packages, and also personal
work. We are sure that it is a great visual
trip to this great continent, which has
so much to offer to the whole world.

telles, bewegen sich ihre Arbeiten auf dem
schmalen Grad zwischen kommerziell und
nichtkommerziell.

In vielen Ländern war es schwierig, die
Designer zu erreichen und mit ihnen zu kom-
munizieren. Hier war es somit ein wesentli-
cher Bestandteil unseres Jobs, Kontakte zu
Fachleuten und Beratern aufzubauen. Vieler-
orts waren wir daher auf die Kooperation mit
den fähigsten Fachleuten und Lehrkräften
für Design angewiesen, um die jeweilige
Designlandschaft bestmöglich abzudecken.
Das Ergebnis ist diese äußerst anregende
Mischung der Kulturen, die in faszinierenden
Plakaten, Buch- und Zeitschriftengestaltun-
gen, Logos, Broschüren, Branding-Projekten,
Verpackungen und auch persönlichen Arbeiten umgesetzt wurde. Wir sind überzeugt,
dass es eine großartige visuelle Reise zu
diesem bedeutenden Kontinent ist, der der
ganzen Welt so viel zu bieten hat.

de joindre des professionnels et des conseill-
ers. Nous avons fait appel à une grande
partie des professionnels et spécialistes en
design les plus doués dans bien des pays,
afin d'avoir un regard le plus complet possible. Le résultat donne un mélange stimulant
de cultures, qui se traduit dans de fabuleux
design d'affiches, de livres et de magazines,
des logos, des brochures, des projets de
branding, des emballages et des travaux
personnels. Nous sommes convaincus qu'il
s'agit d'un merveilleux voyage visuel à
travers ce formidable continent qui a tant
de choses à offrir au reste du monde.

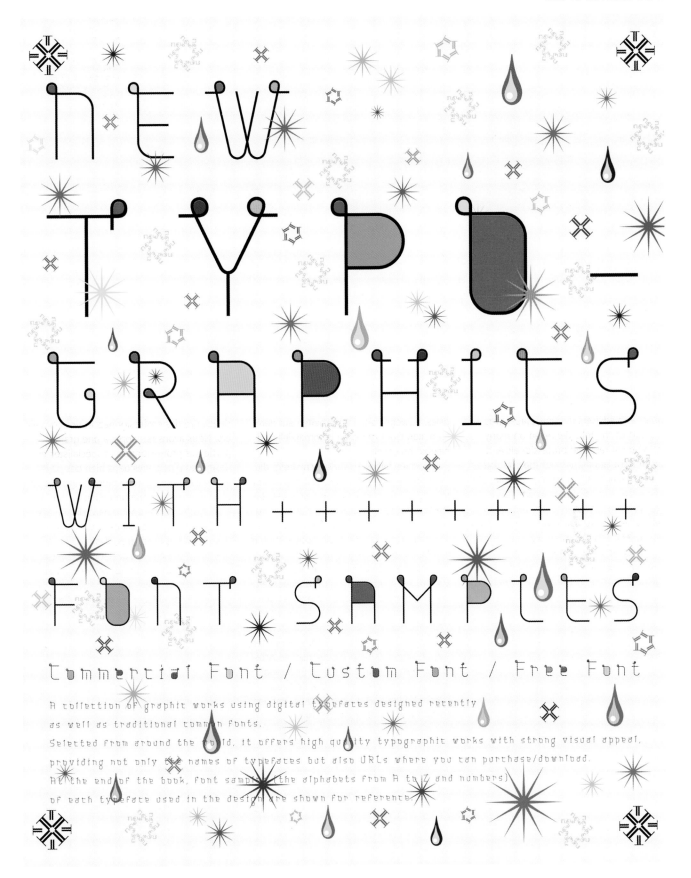

NEW TYPO-GRAPHICS

WITH +++++++++ FONT SAMPLES

Commercial Font / Custom Font / Free Font

A collection of graphic works using digital typefaces designed recently as well as traditional common fonts.

Selected from around the world, it offers high quality typographic works with strong visual appeal, providing not only the names of typefaces but also URLs where you can purchase/download.

At the end of the book, font samples (the alphabets from A to Z and numbers) of each typeface used in the design are shown for reference.

THE CURRENT STATE OF CHINESE DESIGN

by Min Wang

Min Wang was born in China where he began his studies, before moving to Germany, Switzerland, and the United States, countries where he has studied and worked for twenty years. An AGI member and former Vice-President of Icograda, he was appointed Design Director for the 2008 Beijing Olympic Games. Currently he is Dean of the School of Design at China Central Academy of Fine Arts (CAFA) in Beijing, and Design Director of Square Two Design.

I was taking a walk in Beijing yesterday with Erik Spiekermann, a German designer. It was Erik's first time in China and everything was fresh for him. After half a day he declared that Beijing is rather developed with many examples of modern architecture and clean streets, so why does the German government still regard China as a developing country? I told him that China is a vast country with development sharply unbalanced between the big cities in the east and the many underdeveloped inland regions, and with the country in a process of fast development a holistic image of China cannot be obtained based on superficial and local observations, or it will be like the blind men feeling the elephant.

Today I am asked to write 1,000 words on the current state of Chinese design, and I am worried that what I describe may be some lo-

Min Wang wurde in China geboren, wo er sein Studium aufnahm, bevor er nach Deutschland, in die Schweiz und in die USA ging und dort zwanzig Jahre studierte und arbeitete. Er ist Mitglied der AGI und war Vizepräsident der Icograda. Für die Olympischen Spiele 2008 in Beijing wurde er zum Design Director ernannt. Derzeit ist er Dekan der Schule für Gestaltung der China Central Academy of Fine Arts (CAFA) in Beijing und Design Director bei Square Two Design.

Gestern spazierte ich mit dem deutschen Designer Erik Spiekermann durch Beijing. Erik war zum ersten Mal in China, für ihn war alles neu. Nach einem halben Tag stellte er fest, dass Beijing mit seinen vielen Beispielen moderner Architektur und den sauberen Straßen ziemlich entwickelt ist, und fragte mich, warum die deutsche Regierung China immer noch als Entwicklungsland betrachtet. Ich erklärte ihm, dass China ein riesiges Land ist, in dem die Entwicklung zwischen den großen Städten im Osten und den vielen unterentwickelten Regionen im Landesinneren deutlich unausgewogen ist, und dass man sich aufgrund oberflächlicher, lokal begrenzter Beobachtungen kein ganzheitliches Bild von diesem Land machen kann, das sich in einem rasanten Umbruch befindet. Ansonsten wäre es wie in dem Gleichnis von den Blinden, die einen Elefanten betasten.

Min Wang est né en Chine, où il a commencé ses études avant de s'installer en Allemagne, en Suisse et aux États-Unis, pays où il a poursuivi ses études et travaillé pendant vingt ans. Membre de l'AGI et ancien vice-président d'Icograda, il a été choisi comme directeur du design pour les Jeux olympiques de 2008 à Beijing. Il est actuellement directeur de l'école de design à la China Central Academy of Fine Arts (CAFA) à Beijing, ainsi que directeur du design chez Square Two Design.

Je me promenais hier dans Beijing avec Erik Spiekermann, un designer allemand. C'est la première fois qu'Erik vient en Chine et tout était nouveau pour lui. Après une demi-journée, il a conclu que Beijing était une ville plutôt développée, avec de nombreux exemples d'architecture moderne et des rues propres, et il s'est demandé pourquoi le gouvernement allemand considérait la Chine comme un pays encore en voie de développement. Je lui ai expliqué que la Chine est un pays gigantesque au développement très inégal entre les grandes villes de l'Est et les nombreuses régions intérieures sous-développées. Dans un pays en phase de développement rapide comme la Chine, une image holistique ne s'obtient pas sur des observations superficielles et locales, pour ne pas faire comme dans l'histoire des aveugles et de l'éléphant.

Olympic Stamps
Beijing 2008 Olympic
Games, China

cal phenomena rather than a whole picture of the design scene. In the words of the Chinese artist Ai Weiwei, China is like a birthday cake cut open: in each layer one finds something different. What I present here is but some cream and different fruits, and please do not take them as the cake itself.

There are so many designers in China. Nearly one million students have taken design courses at college, and as far as I know there are no statistics for the number of practising designers, which must indeed be huge.

Young Chinese designers are very active on the international stage. More and more of their works are seen in design competitions and exhibitions. Some of them are internationally recognised, even first-rate internationals, and more will emerge on the international design scene.

Design as a profession is no longer a desired high-income option. With large numbers of designers now in the business, market competition has driven the income of Chinese designers to the corresponding social level of their European-American counterparts (not the absolute income), whereas a decade or so ago design was a top-ten most-desired high-income profession for young people.

Chinese designers show very strong learning and receptive abilities. Some thirty

Man hat mich gebeten, 1000 Wörter zum aktuellen Stand des chinesischen Designs zu verfassen, und ich habe nun Angst, nur ein lokales Phänomen zu beschreiben, anstatt ein umfassendes Bild der Designszene zu zeichnen. Der chinesische Künstler Ai Weiwei drückt es so aus: China ist wie ein Geburtstagskuchen, den man anschneidet: In jeder Schicht findet man etwas anderes. Was ich im Folgenden vorstelle, ist nur etwas Sahne und verschiedene Früchte. Bitte missverstehen Sie das nicht als den eigentlichen Kuchen.

Es gibt unglaublich viele Designer in China: Fast eine Million Studierende belegen an den Fach- und Hochschulen Designkurse. Meines Wissens gibt es aber keine Statistik über die Zahl der beruflich als Designer tätigen Personen, die allerdings riesig sein muss.

Junge chinesische Designer sind auf der internationalen Bühne sehr aktiv. Immer mehr Arbeiten werden bei Designwettbewerben und in Ausstellungen gezeigt. Manche sind international bekannt, gehören weltweit sogar zur ersten Riege, und viele weitere werden noch in der internationalen Designszene erscheinen.

Der Beruf des Designers ist in China nicht länger eine begehrte Option auf ein hohes Einkommen. Da es von Designern nur so wimmelt, hat sich deren Einkommen durch

Je dois aujourd'hui écrire 1000 mots sur l'état actuel du design chinois, et je crains que ma description corresponde à un phénomène local sans offrir l'image complète du secteur. Pour citer l'artiste chinois Ai Weiwei, la Chine est comme un gâteau d'anniversaire coupé : chaque couche montre quelque chose de différent. J'explique ici un peu de crème et quelques fruits, à ne pas prendre pour le gâteau en soi.

La Chine compte une foule de designers. Près d'un million d'étudiants ont suivi des cours de design au lycée et si mes données sont bonnes, il n'existe pas de statistiques du nombre de designers en exercice, qui doit être énorme.

Les jeunes designers chinois sont très actifs sur la scène internationale. Leurs travaux sont de plus en plus en vue lors de compétitions et d'expositions de design. Certains jouissent d'une renommée mondiale, voire d'une position de premier ordre, et bien d'autres sont en passe de s'imposer à leur tour.

Cette profession n'est plus une option choisie comme garantie de bons revenus. Avec une foule de designers à présent sur le marché, la concurrence a fait passer les designers chinois au même niveau social que leurs homologues européens et américains (pas le salaire absolu), alors qu'il y a encore

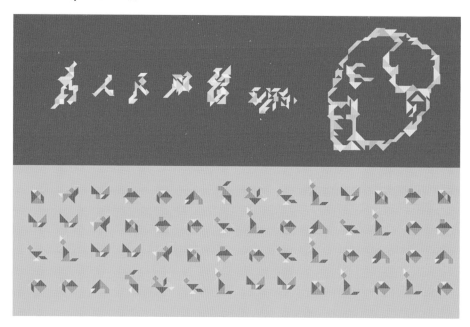

years ago design work here was so isolated from the rest of the world that one could say there was hardly any design – design was needed everywhere. In a very short time, however, Chinese designers refreshed the look of the country – although in some places too much, in others inadequately, and others again with mixed signals, yet generally speaking the achievements were remarkable. The great progress of Chinese design in recent years is noticeable everywhere, from book design, VI design, and information design to display design.

The Icograda World Design Congress in Beijing in 2009 was a highly significant event in Chinese design. Hosted by the China Central Academy of Fine Arts, the Congress elevated the exchanges between Chinese and international designers to a new platform and a new context.

What is regrettable though is that there is not a national association of graphic designers in China. Of the several local organisations, Shenzhen Graphic Design Association (SGDA) turns out to be the most active one. Without a national association, the overall voice of the business is inevitably absent, as too are the formulation and supervision of professional conduct and the demand and action for the promotion of professional standards.

den Wettbewerb auf einem Niveau eingependelt, das sozial (nicht nach absolutem Einkommen) dem ihrer europäisch-amerikanischen KollegInnen entspricht. Noch vor etwa zehn Jahren gehörte dieser Arbeitsbereich bei jungen Leuten zu den Top Ten der begehrtesten und bestbezahlten Berufe.

Chinesische Designer zeigen, wie lern- und aufnahmefähig sie sind. Vor etwa dreißig Jahren war Design hier von der restlichen Welt so isoliert, dass man kaum davon sprechen konnte. Es mangelte überall an Gestaltung. Dann allerdings frischten chinesische Designer das Aussehen ihres Landes in kürzester Zeit auf: Obwohl sie hier und da übertrieben, die Gestaltung bisweilen unangemessen ausfiel oder manchmal wahllos zusammengewürfelt wirkte, waren die Ergebnisse insgesamt doch recht bemerkenswert. Der große Fortschritt des chinesischen Designs in den letzten Jahren ist überall spürbar: von der Buchgestaltung und visuellen Leitsystemen über das Informationsdesign bis hin zum Display-Design.

Der Weltdesignkongress Icograda fand 2009 in Beijing statt und war für das chinesische Design ein höchst signifikantes Ereignis. Gastgeber war die China Central Academy of Fine Arts. Dieser Kongress führte zu einer neuartigen Ebene des Austausches zwischen chinesischen und internationalen Designern und stellte einen neuen Kontext her.

une décennie, le design était l'une des dix professions les mieux rémunérées et les plus prisées parmi les jeunes.

Les designers chinois possèdent d'excellentes capacités d'apprentissage et de réceptivité. Il y a 30 ans environ, le design y était tellement isolé du reste du monde qu'il paraissait quasiment absent : il était donc nécessaire partout. En très peu de temps pourtant, les designers chinois ont rafraîchi le look du pays, trop à certains endroits, de façon inappropriée à d'autres, et mal résolu à d'autres encore ; pourtant, les résultats sont dans l'ensemble remarquables. La grande avancée du design chinois ces dernières années s'apprécie partout : design de livres, design d'images virtuelles, design d'informations et design d'affichage.

L'Icograda World Design Congress qui s'est tenu à Beijing en 2009 a constitué un événement de grande envergure pour le design chinois. Dans les installations de la China Central Academy of Fine Arts, le congrès a placé les échanges entre designers chinois et internationaux sur une nouvelle plate-forme et dans un nouveau contexte.

Seul point à déplorer, il n'existe pas d'association au niveau national de designers graphiques en Chine. Parmi les différentes organisations locales, Shenzhen Graphic Design Association (SGDA) s'avère être la plus

Chinese Type Design
poster, 2002, by Ling
Meng, China

*Prohibition of Tobacco;
A Counterblaste to
Tobacco*
poster series, 2009,
by Min Wang, China

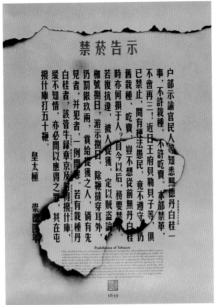

And unfortunately Chinese graphic designers often have to design on spec. Although Icograda and many national design associations speak out against design on spec, since clients in China are used to choosing designers by way of spec work, and designers themselves either do not know its potential hazards or only consider their own interests, design on spec is still justified, and this too underlines the need for a national association of graphic designers in China.

With China on the track of fast development and with different regions in different stages of development, now is really a good time for designers to play their role.

Leider gibt es in China keinen nationalen Verband der Grafikdesigner. Von den verschiedenen lokalen Organisationen ist die Shenzhen Graphic Design Association (SGDA) die aktivste. Ohne nationale Interessenvertretung fehlt der gesamten Branche jedoch eine Stimme, auch hinsichtlich der Formulierung und der Überwachung von berufs- und standesgemäßen Regeln sowie der Forderung, professionelle Standards zu schaffen und aktiv zu fördern.

Und bedauerlicherweise müssen chinesische Grafikdesigner oft Aufträge als „Spec Work" annehmen. Das heißt, sie erbringen Leistungen im Voraus und müssen darauf spekulieren, ein Honorar zu bekommen. Obwohl sich Icograda und viele nationale Designverbände gegen ein „Design on spec" aussprechen, sind chinesische Kunden daran gewöhnt, Designer anhand gestalterischer Vorleistungen auszuwählen. Und entweder erkennen die Designer selbst nicht die damit verbundene potenzielle Gefahr oder sie denken nur an ihre eigenen Interessen. Deshalb ist „Spec Work" nach wie vor weit verbreitet, was den Bedarf an einer nationalen Interessenvertretung zusätzlich unterstreicht.

Wegen der schnellen Entwicklung Chinas und weil sich die verschiedenen Regionen in unterschiedlichen Entwicklungsphasen befinden, ist jetzt genau der richtige Zeitpunkt für die Designer, ihre Rolle auszufüllen.

active. Sans une entité nationale, aucune voix globale du secteur ne se fait entendre. Autres grands absents : l'expression et le contrôle de la conduite professionnelle, ainsi que la demande et des initiatives de promotion des normes de la profession.

Malheureusement aussi, les designers graphiques chinois doivent souvent travailler sans contrat. Même si Icograda et de nombreuses autres associations nationales de design s'y opposent, sachant que les clients en Chine sont habitués à choisir des designers sans contrat et que les propres designers ne connaissent pas les risques potentiels liés ou ne pensent qu'à leurs intérêts, le design sans contrat continue à se justifier. Ce point souligne là encore le besoin d'une association nationale de designers graphiques.

La Chine est dans une phase de progression rapide et ses régions se trouvent à des niveaux distincts de développement. Le moment est opportun pour que les designers y jouent un rôle.

a foreign eye

by Bruno Porto

Bruno Porto was born in Rio de Janeiro, and is a graphic designer, educator, and author, with work widely published. He has received various awards and had his work exhibited in the Americas, Europe, and Asia. A former director of the Brazilian Graphic Designers Association, ADG Brasil, he regularly takes part in and organises design congresses, lectures, awards juries, workshops, and exhibitions around the world. He collaborates frequently with Chinese design magazines Art & Design and NewGraphic, and presently teaches at the Raffles Design Institute in Shanghai, where he currently lives.

Bruno Porto wurde in Rio de Janeiro geboren. Der Grafikdesigner, Pädagoge und Autor zahlreicher Veröffentlichungen wurde mit verschiedenen Preisen ausgezeichnet, seine Arbeiten wurden in Nord- und Südamerika sowie in Europa und Asien gezeigt. Als ehemaliger Direktor der brasilianischen Graphic Designers Association ADG Brasil organisiert er und beteiligt sich auch regelmäßig an Designkongressen, Vorträgen, Wettbewerbsjurys, Workshops und Ausstellungen in der ganzen Welt. Er arbeitet häufig mit den chinesischen Designmagazinen Art & Design und NewGraphic zusammen. Derzeit unterrichtet er am Raffles Design Institute in Shanghai, wo er auch lebt.

Bruno Porto est né à Rio de Janeiro et est designer graphique, éducateur et auteur, ses travaux étant largement publiés. Il a reçu plusieurs prix et ses œuvres ont été présentées en Amérique, en Europe et en Asie. Ancien directeur de l'association des designers graphiques du Brésil, ADG Brasil, il fait régulièrement des participations et organise à travers le monde des congrès, des conférences, des jurys, des ateliers et des expositions liés au design. Il collabore souvent avec les magazines de design chinois Art & Design et NewGraphic, et il enseigne actuellement au Raffles Design Institute de Shanghai, où il réside.

Casting a foreign eye on present-day Asian graphics is almost as fascinating as being in Asia itself. Like any trip, it is better enjoyed if one knows a few facts (not necessarily historical ones, although that helps too) before arriving. First, one must dismiss any twisted perception of all Asian graphics being one single voice, like predictably stacked sinographs, warm colours or cute mascots (although there are plenty of these). The keyword here should be *countless*, and its like.

Be ready to embrace the abundance of typefaces in dozens of languages, and how they can be arranged in the most astounding layouts. Keep in mind that symbols, colour palettes, and other signs that may be

Betrachtet man als Ausländer zeitgenössische asiatische Grafik, ist das ähnlich faszinierend wie ein Aufenthalt in Asien selbst. Wie auf jeder Reise ist der Genuss auch in diesem Fall intensiver, wenn man ein paar Fakten kennt (nicht notwendigerweise historische, obwohl auch das hilfreich ist), noch bevor man den Ausgangspunkt erreicht. Zunächst einmal sollte man sich von der Vorstellung verabschieden, asiatische Grafik sei aus einem Guss – wie vorhersagbar zusammengefügte chinesische Schriftzeichen, warme Farben oder niedliche Maskottchen (obwohl es davon sehr viele gibt). Das Schlüsselwort hier ist *zahllos* oder eines seiner Synonyme.

Si l'on pose un regard étranger sur le graphisme asiatique du moment, l'expérience est presque aussi fascinante qu'un séjour en Asie. Comme tout voyage, le plaisir est accru quand on dispose de quelques données (pas forcément historiques, même si c'est utile) avant l'arrivée. Il faut d'abord abandonner toute perception fausse que l'ensemble du graphisme asiatique est une voix unique, avec ses files de sinogrammes, ses couleurs chaudes ou ses adorables mascottes (bien que tous abondent). Le mot clé pour les éléments graphiques doit être *innombrable* (ou équivalent).

Préparez-vous à découvrir l'abondance de caractères dans des dizaines de langues, et la

Read
poster, 2008,
by Hwan uk Choe,
Hanuku, South Korea

commonplace to you, carry different (or no) meanings here. Mascots and morphological pictograms are not to be seen only as entertainment or trademark licensing characters, but often as a strategy to accessibly communicate with uneducated audiences. You may find yourself somewhat acquainted with projects or brands in this book, but not necessarily within the same context. Consider that Asian designers may be conveying messages that are totally unrelated to your culture, habits or society. Or the exact opposite: they might be promoting products and services that are yet to be assimilated by their target audiences.

Because of economical and political circumstances – that lead to distinct technological and cultural facets – Asian nations are in various stages of design development. In some countries, for example, it was not so easy to locate all genres – packaging, branding, advertising, etc. – of graphic design. China, one of the leading countries in the world, has over 100,000 advertising agencies of all shapes and sizes, but advertising only commenced here some thirty years ago, with the relaxation of government control over communications.

Perhaps because of a strong pictorial tradition in the arts, the boundaries between graphic design and illustration

Bereiten Sie sich auf eine Fülle von Schriftsystemen in Dutzenden von Sprachen vor und auf die erstaunlichsten Layouts, die sich damit gestalten lassen. Bedenken Sie, dass Symbole, Farben und andere Zeichen, die Ihnen vertraut sein mögen, hier andere (oder gar keine) Bedeutungen haben. Maskottchen und Piktogramme sollten nicht nur als lizenzierte Figuren von Handelsmarken betrachtet werden, die der Unterhaltung dienen, sondern auch als Strategie, um niedrigschwellig mit ungeschulten Zielgruppen zu kommunizieren. Bestimmte Projekte oder Marken in diesem Buch könnten Ihnen vertraut vorkommen, stehen aber nicht notwendigerweise in ihrem gewohnten Kontext. Bedenken Sie, dass asiatische Designer Botschaften vermitteln wollen, die in Ihrer Kultur, aufgrund Ihrer Gewohnheiten oder in Ihrer Gesellschaft in einem ganz anderen Zusammenhang stehen. Oder andersherum: Vielleicht bewerben asiatische Designer Produkte und Dienstleistungen, die von ihrem Zielpublikum erst noch assimiliert werden müssen.

Aufgrund der ökonomischen und politischen Umstände – die zu klar unterscheidbaren technologischen und kulturellen Facetten führen – sind asiatische Nationen hinsichtlich des Designs in verschiedenen Entwicklungsphasen. In manchen Ländern war es beispielsweise nicht so einfach, alle Genres

façon dont ils s'organisent dans les compositions les plus époustouflantes. N'oubliez pas que les symboles, les palettes de couleurs et autres signes ordinaires à vos yeux peuvent avoir ici d'autres significations (ou aucune). Les mascottes et les pictogrammes morphologiques ne doivent pas uniquement être associés à des distractions ou des marques; ils renferment souvent une stratégie pour atteindre facilement des publics non instruits. Vous connaîtrez peut-être certains projets ou marques présents dans cet ouvrage, mais pas forcément dans le même contexte. Pensez que les designers asiatiques peuvent transmettre des messages sans aucune relation avec votre culture, vos habitudes ou votre société. Ou bien tout l'inverse : ils peuvent promouvoir des produits et des services que les publics cibles doivent encore assimiler.

En raison de la conjoncture économique et politique, qui donne une variété de facettes technologiques et culturelles, les nations asiatiques se trouvent à des phases différentes de développement en termes de design. Dans certains pays par exemple, il n'a pas été simple de trouver tous les genres de design graphique (emballages, branding, publicité, etc.). La Chine, l'un des pays leaders au monde, compte plus de 100 000 agences de publicité de toutes forme et de toute taille, alors que la publicité n'a vu le jour qu'il y a

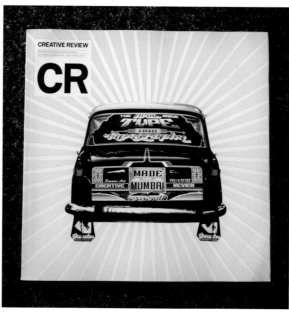

in many Asian cultures overlap to a point where a great deal of professionals (let alone students) seem to confuse the two. Portfolios and publications often feature a great deal of illustration-only projects (like sketchbooks), personal or installation art, and even plain photography labelled as "Graphic Design". Some breathtaking work, for sure, but not really design. On the other hand, the most design-mature countries present plenty of first-rate companies, providing every aspect of graphic design services anyone might need.

Regarding graphic-design development, I am truly convinced that the Internet – although heavily censored for over 25 % of the planet – plays a bigger role here than on any of the other continents. It vehemently became this modern (and rather chaotic) Library of Alexandria turned into a publishing house (and bookstore, for that matter). Like everywhere else, it allows experienced companies and young talent to publish and promote their work, and it facilitates a promiscuous exchange of references. But, in Asia, as a consequence of the enormous amount of people and their both shared and differing cultural grounds and alphabets, all of this progresses exponentially. It is delightful to see Malaysian freelancers working for Chinese clients,

des Grafikdesigns wie Verpackung, Branding, Werbung etc. abgedeckt zu finden. China ist eine der führenden Nationen dieser Welt und verfügt über mehr als 100.000 Werbeagenturen in allen denkbaren Formen und Größen, doch Werbung im eigentlichen Sinne fasste hier erst vor etwa dreißig Jahren Fuß, als die Regierung die strikten Auflagen für Kommunikationsformen lockerte.

Es mag an der stark bildlich verhafteten Tradition der Künste liegen, dass die Grenzen zwischen Grafikdesign und Illustration in vielen asiatischen Kulturen verwischen. So stark, dass ein Großteil der Fachleute (ganz zu schweigen von den Studierenden) beides scheinbar nicht mehr auseinanderhalten kann. Portfolios und Publikationen bestehen häufig zu einem großen Teil aus reinen Illustrations-Projekten (wie Skizzenbüchern), aus eigenen künstlerischen Arbeiten oder Kunst-Installationen und sogar lediglich aus Fotografien, die dann als „Grafikdesign" etikettiert werden. Manchmal gute Arbeiten, aber kein Design im eigentlichen Sinne. Andererseits verfügen viele Länder über eine Vielzahl erstklassiger Firmen, die jeden beliebigen Aspekt in Hinblick auf das Grafikdesign abdecken.

Was die Entwicklung des Grafikdesigns angeht, bin ich fest davon überzeugt, dass das Internet, obwohl es in über einem Viertel der Welt stark zensiert wird, hier eine größere

une trentaine d'années, grâce à l'assouplissement du contrôle des communications par le gouvernement.

En raison peut-être d'une tradition picturale ancrée dans les arts, la frontière entre le design graphique et l'illustration est floue dans bien des cultures asiatiques, au point qu'un grand nombre de professionnels (sans parler des étudiants) semblent confondre les deux. Les portfolios et les publications présentent souvent quantité de projets exclusivement d'illustration (comme des carnets à dessins), des œuvres personnelles ou des installations, voire des photographies, le tout avec l'étiquette « design graphique ». Des travaux certes formidables, mais qui n'ont pas franchement à voir avec le design. Par ailleurs, les pays les plus mûrs en design comptent de nombreuses entreprises de premier ordre, couvrant tous les aspects des services de design graphique qu'une personne peut rechercher.

Concernant le développement du design graphique, je suis totalement convaincu qu'Internet, bien que censuré dans plus de 25 % de la planète, y joue un rôle plus important que sur n'importe quel autre continent. Il s'est imposé comme une bibliothèque d'Alexandrie moderne (et assez chaotique) transformée en maison d'édition (et librairie, pour l'occasion). Comme partout ailleurs, il permet aux entreprises confir-

Creative Review Cover
magazine cover, 2009, by
Grandmother India Design,
India

Design School India
logo, 2009, by Ishan Khosla
Design, India

multinational agencies with subsidiaries in Singapore, Hong Kong, and Thailand doing business along with Australian partners, Taiwanese poster designers being celebrated in South America, or Korean design students collaborating with a Japanese magazine.

At a continually increasing rate, a large proportion of these professionals work beyond borders, both geographically and metaphorically. Especially in the last decade, design in Asia has been experiencing firsthand the results of an ongoing globalisation. In this new world, many Asian designers are being trained – initially in agencies, but now while still in school – to conceive bilingual packages, publications, and identity systems. This obviously doesn't happen only within Asian borders. "East meets West" brings consequences to Asian graphic design and raises a few questions.

Is *Asian Graphics Now!* a book about graphic design "Made in Asia" or "made by Asian designers"? It was a simple but tough question to answer. Julius Wiedemann, Daniel Siciliano Bretas, Sadao Maekawa and I kept discussing it throughout the months this book was being developed. Mostly through several Skype meetings – with me living in China, Sadao in Japan, Daniel in Germany, and Julius everywhere (really!) –

Rolle spielt als auf jedem anderen Kontinent. Es entwickelte sich zu dieser modernen (und recht chaotischen) Variante der Bibliothek von Alexandria, die sich dann zu einem Verlag (und auch zu einer Buchhandlung) verwandelte. Überall erlaubt das Internet erfahrenen Firmen und jungen Talenten, ihre Arbeiten zu veröffentlichen und für sie zu werben, und erleichtert darüber hinaus einen regen Austausch von Referenzen. In Asien hat das zur Folge, dass die Entwicklung angesichts der enormen Menschenmassen mit ihren sowohl gemeinsamen als auch unterschiedlichen kulturellen Wurzeln und Alphabeten exponentiell voranschreitet: Freiberufler aus Malaysia arbeiten für chinesische Kunden, multinationale Agenturen mit Filialen in Singapur, Hongkong oder Thailand tätigen ihre Geschäfte mit australischen Partnern, Plakatgestalter aus Taiwan werden in Südamerika gefeiert, und koreanische Designstudenten arbeiten für ein japanisches Magazin.

Ein immer größerer Teil dieser Fachleute arbeitet grenzüberschreitend – was sowohl geografisch als auch metaphorisch gemeint ist. Vor allem im vergangenen Jahrzehnt hat das asiatische Design die Folgen der fortschreitenden Globalisierung aus erster Hand erfahren. In dieser neuen Welt werden viele asiatische Designer ausgebildet, um zweisprachige Verpackungen, Publikationen und Iden-

mées et aux jeunes talents de publier et de promouvoir leur travail, tout en offrant un échange libre de références. Mais en Asie, en raison du nombre très élevé d'habitants, ainsi que d'un bagage culturel et d'alphabets à la fois partagés et différents, tout ceci connaît une croissance exponentielle. Il est bon de voir que des freelances malaisiens travaillent pour des clients chinois, que des agences multinationales avec des filiales à Singapour, à Hong Kong et en Thaïlande s'associent à des partenaires australiens, que des designers d'affiches taïwanais sont reconnus en Amérique du Sud, ou que des étudiants de design coréens collaborent à un magazine japonais.

Bonne partie de ces professionnels travaillent chaque fois plus au-delà des frontières, tant au niveau géographique que métaphorique. Au cours de la dernière décennie notamment, le design en Asie a connu de première main les effets d'une globalisation continue. Dans ce nouveau monde, de nombreux designers asiatiques sont formés (avant dans des agences, maintenant quand ils sont encore en train d'étudier) pour concevoir des emballages, des publications et des systèmes d'identité bilingues. Le phénomène ne se produit évidemment pas seulement à l'intérieur des frontières asiatiques. Le concept « L'Est rencontre l'Ouest »

but also in a few face-to-face opportunities in China and Japan. It never got an easy answer, and it got even harder when we started looking at the submitted projects.

As the title suggests, the objective of this book is to feature the contemporary graphic design one may find in Asia, and yes, made by Asian designers. But is this still possible, or accurate, in contemporary Asia?

Globalisation has Asian designers working for clients in other continents (sometimes even residing there), and yet using the same skills, tools, and visual styles developed in their home countries. Simultaneously, every major Western advertising agency owns its local branch in Asian countries. Some, actually, have been here for the last two decades. Many of these offices have Western senior designers and art directors either supervising the work of local staff, or doing the jobs themselves, for Asian clients.

Still, we aimed mainly at two concepts: graphic design found in Asia, made by Asian designers. But that doesn't mean that the book avoided Asian professionals who are doing great work abroad. Nor did it suppress great work that is seen in Asian streets, supermarkets, bookstores, and even art galleries, but which was designed by teams with non Asia-born members in it.

titätssysteme zu konzipieren – anfangs noch in Agenturen, aber heute schon während sie noch die Schule besuchen. Das passiert natürlich nicht nur innerhalb der asiatischen Grenzen. „Ost trifft West" wirkt sich auf das asiatische Grafikdesign aus und wirft so manche Frage auf.

Ist *Asian Graphics Now!* ein Buch über „Grafikdesign made in Asia" oder über „Grafikdesign von asiatischen Designern"? Eine einfache Frage, die schwer zu beantworten ist. Julius Wiedemann, Daniel Siciliano Bretas, Sadao Maekawa und ich haben das in den Monaten, in denen wir dieses Buch entwickelten, vor allem im Rahmen von Skype-Meetings diskutiert: Ich lebe in China, Sadao in Japan, Daniel in Deutschland und Julius praktisch überall (wirklich!). Aber wir trafen uns auch ein paar Mal persönlich in China und Japan. Auf diese Frage fanden wir keine einfache Antwort, und es wurde noch schwerer, als wir uns die eingereichten Projekte anschauten.

Wie der Titel nahelegt, stellt dieses Buch das aktuelle Grafikdesign in Asien vor, das – genau, richtig! – von asiatischen Designern produziert wurde. Aber ist das im gegenwärtigen Asien überhaupt noch möglich – oder zutreffend?

Durch die Globalisierung arbeiten asiatische Designer für Kunden auf anderen Kontinenten (und manchmal leben sie auch dort), nutzen

a des conséquences sur le design graphique asiatique et pose plusieurs questions.

L'ouvrage *Asian Graphics Now!* traite-t-il du design graphique « Made in Asia » ou fait par des designers asiatiques ? La question était délicate. Julius Wiedemann, Daniel Siciliano Bretas, Sadao Maekawa et moi-même en avons parlé pendant les mois d'élaboration du livre sur Skype (j'habite en Chine, Sadao au Japon, Daniel en Allemagne et Julius un peu partout, littéralement !), mais également face à face en Chine et au Japon. Nous ne sommes jamais parvenu à une réponse simple, encore moins quand nous avons commencé à étudier les projets proposés.

Comme le titre l'indique, l'objectif de l'ouvrage est de montrer le design graphique contemporain que l'on trouve en Asie et, en effet, œuvre de designers asiatiques. Tout ceci est-il possible ou exact dans l'Asie actuelle ?

Avec la globalisation, certains designers asiatiques travaillent pour des clients sur d'autres continents (eux-mêmes y résident parfois), tout en faisant appel aux mêmes compétences, outils et styles visuels développés dans leur pays natal. En parallèle, toutes les principales agences de publicité occidentales possèdent une filiale locale dans des pays d'Asie. Certaines y sont mêmes présentes depuis deux décennies. Nombre de ces bureaux ont des designers seniors

After all, this is a careful yet generous portrait of a fast, exciting, ever-changing reality that keeps evolving.

Still, there remains the persistent cliché that won't go away: what are the characteristics of Asian graphic design in our times? We are hoping this book provides an answer.

aber die Fertigkeiten, Tools und visuellen Stile, die sie in ihren Heimatländern entwickelt haben. Gleichzeitig verfügt jede große westliche Werbeagentur über eigene lokale Niederlassungen in Asien. Manche sind schon über zwei Jahrzehnte am Markt. Viele dieser Büros werden von westlichen Designern und Art Directors geleitet, die entweder die Arbeiten der heimischen Mitarbeiter überwachen oder selbst für asiatische Auftraggeber arbeiten.

Wir zielen allerdings hauptsächlich auf zwei Aspekte: ein aus Asien stammendes Grafikdesign, das von asiatischen Designern produziert wurde. Das bedeutet jedoch nicht, dass das Buch Fachleute aus Asien außer Acht lässt, die im Ausland großartige Arbeiten abliefern. Es fallen auch nicht unter den Tisch die einzigartigen Arbeiten, die man in den Straßen, Supermärkten, Buchläden oder gar Kunstgalerien in ganz Asien sieht, die aber von Teams gestaltet wurden, in denen auch außerhalb Asiens geborene Mitglieder tätig sind. So ist dies ein sorgfältig recherchiertes und dennoch großzügiges Porträt einer schnellen, spannenden und sich ständig ändernden Realität geworden, die sich weiter entwickelt.

Es bleibt jedoch ein allgemeines Klischee, das sich einfach nicht abschütteln lässt: Was sind die Merkmale des asiatischen Grafikdesigns in unserer heutigen Zeit? Wir hoffen, dass dieses Buch eine Antwort darauf liefert.

et des directeurs artistiques occidentaux qui supervisent le travail du personnel local ou se chargent eux-mêmes des projets pour des clients asiatiques.

Dans tous les cas, nous nous sommes concentrés sur deux concepts : le design graphique présent en Asie, fait par des designers asiatiques. L'ouvrage n'ignore pas pour autant les professionnels asiatiques qui excellent à l'étranger, pas plus que les œuvres de qualité dans les rues, les supermarchés, les librairies, voire les galeries d'art en Asie, mais qui ont été conçues par des équipes dont aucun membre n'est originaire d'Asie. Il s'agit donc là d'un portrait soigné et généreux à la fois d'une réalité dynamique, passionnante et changeant sans cesse.

Il n'en demeure pas moins un cliché pesant : quelles sont les caractéristiques du design graphique asiatique à l'heure actuelle ? Nous espérons que cet ouvrage apportera une réponse.

CHINA'S PACKAGING DESIGN

by Huang Li

Huang Li is the editor and publisher of Package & Design, a professional design magazine with great influence in China. Born in Guangdong, he is a graduate from the Guangzhou Academy of Fine Arts and has practised for many years as a packaging and graphic designer, winning awards that include the World Star of Packaging from the World Packaging Organization.

Huang Li ist Redakteur und Herausgeber von Package & Design, einer Fachzeitschrift für Design mit großem Einfluss in China. Er wurde in Guangdong geboren und hat seinen Abschluss an der Guangzhou Academy of Fine Arts gemacht. Er verfügt über langjährige Berufserfahrung als Verpackungs- und Grafikdesigner und hat eine Reihe von Preisen gewonnen, darunter den World Star of Packaging der World Packaging Organization.

Huang Li est l'éditeur de Package & Design, un magazine de design professionnel ayant une grande influence en Chine. Né à Guangdong, il est diplômé de l'académie des Beaux-Arts de Guangzhou et a exercé pendant longtemps comme designer d'emballages et graphique, remportant des prix comme le World Star of Packaging de l'organisation mondiale d'emballages.

Today, the development of China's packaging-design industry has become increasingly subject to international trade concerns. Understanding its development process and understanding China's economic development will help us exchange, cooperate, and develop this field.

Looking at recent decades, the development of China's packaging-design industry, although faced with many challenges and difficulties, has been achieved with considerable "sustained high speed", and the process can be summarised in three stages as follows:

The end of the '70s to the mid '80s marked the beginning of a changing era, with the state implementing policies intended to ease communication with other countries. With that, a tremendous change took place in the domestic market, while the import of foreign packaging-design concepts refreshed those known previously

Chinesisches Verpackungsdesign ist heute eine Branche mit zunehmendem Belang für den internationalen Handel. Wenn wir seinen Entwicklungsprozess und den der chinesischen Wirtschaft insgesamt nachvollziehen, hilft uns das, Austausch und Kooperation zu fördern und die Branche weiterzuentwickeln.

Schaut man sich die zurückliegenden Jahrzehnte an, entwickelte sich das chinesische Verpackungsdesign mit beachtlicher und „nachhaltiger Höchstgeschwindigkeit", obwohl die Branche vielen Herausforderungen und Schwierigkeiten trotzen musste. Diesen Prozess kann man in die folgenden drei Phasen unterteilen:

Vom Ende der 70er bis zur Mitte der 80er Jahre des vorigen Jahrhunderts finden wir den Beginn einer sich verändernden Ära, in der vom Staat eingeführte Richtlinien die Kommunikation mit anderen Ländern vereinfachen sollten. Das sorgte auf dem heimischen

Le développement de l'industrie du design d'emballages en Chine est de plus en plus sujet à des questions de commerce international. Comprendre son processus de développement et la croissance économique de la Chine nous aidera à échanger, à collaborer et à développer ce secteur.

Si l'on observe les dernières décennies, le développement du design d'emballages en Chine, bien que confronté à de nombreux défis et difficultés, s'est produit à une rythme considérable. Le processus peut se résumer en trois phases.

La période allant de la fin des années 70 au milieu des années 80 a marqué le début d'une nouvelle ère : l'état a mis en place des règles pour faciliter la communication avec d'autres pays. Grâce à cela, une mutation profonde s'est produite sur le marché national, alors que l'importation de concepts étrangers de design d'emballages a actualisé

Liquor Gift Package Design
by Xia Ke, Guge Dynasty
Brand Design Consultation
Company, China

and related patterns of consumption. Consumers and professionals started to realise the importance and value of packaging, especially for Chinese exported products. In that sense, packaging went from quite a low-quality standard towards a more middle-grade quality, involving industry standardisation, wider use of materials, more structural design, and ultimately packaging design itself. In this period, Chinese products weren't able to enter supermarkets abroad, and the World Packaging Organization worked with China's packaging industry to assist with the development and awareness of higher quality standards, generating a big boost in the field.

From the mid '80s to late '90s the industry underwent fast growth and achieved maturity, resulting from the country's economic strength and the enhancement of manufacturing. In Beijing, Shanghai, Guangzhou, and other large cities, large and small design and advertising companies mushroomed. Guangzhou alone had over 6,000 design firms at this time. Such demands required better educated and trained designers to join the industry. Their achievements then encouraged more Chinese designers to participate in international professional exchanges, with many of them gaining international awards. By the end of the '90s, China's packaging-

Markt für gewaltige Veränderungen, während durch den Import ausländischer Konzepte für das Verpackungsdesign die bekannten Ideen und Konzepte und die damit zusammenhängenden Konsummuster neu belebt wurden. Verbraucher und Fachleute begannen, Bedeutung und Wert von Verpackung zu erkennen, vor allem für chinesische Exportprodukte. In diesem Sinn stiegen die Verpackungsstandards von einer relativ niedrigen auf eine eher im Mittelfeld anzusiedelnde Qualitätsstufe. Damit verbunden waren eine Standardisierung der Industrie, ein breiterer Materialeinsatz und ein deutlicher strukturiertes Design. Letzten Endes wirkte sich das auch auf das Verpackungsdesign selbst aus. In dieser Periode konnten sich chinesische Produkte noch nicht in ausländischen Supermärkten durchsetzen. Die World Packaging Organization arbeitete mit der chinesischen Verpackungsindustrie daran, höhere Qualitätsstandards zu entwickeln und ein Bewusstsein dafür zu schaffen. Das zog einen großen Entwicklungsschub in der Branche nach sich.

Zwischen Mitte der 80er bis Ende der 90er Jahre erlebte die Branche ein schnelles Wachstum und gelangte zu einer Reife, die in der Wirtschaftskraft des Landes und den verbesserten Herstellungsbedingungen wurzelte. In Beijing, Shanghai, Guangzhou und anderen großen Städten schossen kleine und

ceux connus jusqu'alors et liés aux modèles de consommation. Les consommateurs et les professionnels ont commencé à saisir l'importance et la valeur de l'emballage, notamment pour les produits chinois exportés. C'est pourquoi l'emballage est passé d'un standard d'assez faible qualité à une qualité plus moyenne, en impliquant la standardisation du secteur, un emploi plus extensif des matériaux, un design plus structurel et le design à proprement parler des emballages. Pendant cette période, les produits chinois n'ont pas pu être vendus dans les supermarchés à l'étranger, et l'organisation mondiale des emballages a travaillé avec l'industrie chinoise pour favoriser le développement et la prise de conscience des standards de meilleure qualité, d'où un bond en avant dans le domaine.

Du milieu des années 80 à la fin des années 90, l'industrie a connu une croissance rapide et est parvenue à maturité, grâce à la puissance économique du pays et à l'amélioration de la fabrication. À Beijing, à Shanghai, à Guangzhou et dans d'autres grandes villes, des agences petites et grandes de design et de publicité ont vu le jour. Rien qu'à Guangzhou, plus de 6 000 studios de design se sont créés à cette période. Cette demande a supposé l'embauche de designers plus instruits et mieux formés. Leur réussite a encou-

design industry had been awarded 77 international prizes, showing a substantial qualitative leap forward. Without good design, the country wouldn't conquer markets, and this simple reality has been quickly recognised by domestic manufacturers.

From 2000 to the present, the industry has continued to develop. The information age and constant updates in technology have challenged professionals to keep pace with development and innovation. One consequence of that has been the attention paid by the industry to the brand-building process, and the relationship with buyers. The creative process today is less focused on local culture and looks more at international market trends, with a global vision of innovation and international standards. With many international brands selling on the Chinese market, foreign designs have now also been put into Chinese designers' hands. Further cooperation between Chinese and international design firms will enable the market to become even more competitive.

In recent years, the government has given great support to various activities in the design field, formulating policies to enable the industry to develop rapidly, and implementing objectives. Shenzhen City, for instance, was declared "Design Capital" by the United Nations, and many

große Design- und Werbeunternehmen wie Pilze aus dem Boden. Allein Guangzhou hat gegenwärtig über 6000 Designagenturen vorzuweisen. Um diesen Anforderungen gerecht zu werden, bedurfte es besser ausgebildeter und erfahrener Designer. Ihre Leistungen ermutigten wiederum andere chinesische Designer, sich am internationalen fachlichen Austausch zu beteiligen, und viele von ihnen erhielten internationale Preise. Gegen Ende der 90er Jahre war die chinesische Verpackungsdesign-Branche mit 77 internationalen Preisen ausgezeichnet worden, Zeichen für einen substanziellen Sprung nach vorn. Ohne gutes Design würde das Land die Märkte nicht erobern können – das erkannten die heimischen Produzenten sehr schnell.

Seit dem Jahr 2000 hat die Branche in ihrer Entwicklung nicht nachgelassen. Das Informationszeitalter und ständig neue technologische Errungenschaften fordern Fachleute heraus, mit den Entwicklungen und Innovationen Schritt zu halten. Konsequenzen daraus sind die Aufmerksamkeit, die die Branche dem Markenbildungsprozess zollt, und die Beziehung zu den Käufern. Der kreative Prozess ist heutzutage weniger auf eine lokale Kultur fokussiert, sondern bezieht vielmehr internationale Markttrends sowie globale Visionen von Innovation und internationalen Standards mit ein. Da auf dem chinesischen

ragé d'autres designers chinois à participer à des échanges professionnels internationaux, beaucoup remportant des récompenses internationales. À la fin des années 90, l'industrie du design d'emballages en Chine avait remporté 77 prix internationaux, preuve d'une avancée de taille en matière de qualité. Sans bon design, le pays ne gagnerait pas des marchés, et cette simple réalité a été rapidement assimilée par les fabricants nationaux.

Depuis 2000, le secteur poursuit son développement. L'ère de l'information et les progrès constants de la technologie ont poussé les professionnels à tenir le rythme des avancées et des innovations. Entre autres conséquences, le secteur s'est concentré sur le processus de création de marque et sur les relations avec les consommateurs. Aujourd'hui, le processus créatif se centre moins sur la culture locale et s'attache davantage aux tendances des marchés internationaux, avec une vision globale d'innovation et de standards mondiaux. Il y a tellement de marques internationales en vente sur le marché chinois que les designs étrangers sont désormais aussi confiés à des designers chinois. Une coopération accrue entre les agences de design chinoises et internationales permettra au marché d'être chaque fois plus compétitif.

Ces dernières années, le gouvernement a offert un grand soutien à diverses activités

Chinese Medicine Package
by Zhang Xiao-ping, Black
Horse Advertising Co., Ltd.,
China

Teabag Family Package
by Chen Ying-Juan, China

*Health Care Product
Package*
by Han Yu-chun, Yi Pin
Design, China

design activities now receive government funding, with professionals also being directly involved in urban development decision-making.

With China's packaging industry undergoing all these stages, we have reasons to believe that it has very positive prospects for the future and will play an important role in economic globalisation. During this development process a lot of excellent designers in China will certainly emerge as the backbone of the industry. In this book we present a number of vivid projects, which demonstrate how Chinese designers communicate with their clients and customers, and how they extend their ideas to the market.

Markt viele internationale Marken vertreten sind, wurden ausländische Designs nun ebenfalls in die Hände chinesischer Designer gelegt. Die Zusammenarbeit von chinesischen und internationalen Designagenturen wird den Markt noch konkurrenzfähiger machen.

In den vergangenen Jahren hat die Regierung Aktivitäten im Bereich des Designs unterstützt und Richtlinien formuliert, die die Branche in die Lage versetzen, sich rapide zu entwickeln und Zielvorgaben umzusetzen. Shenzhen City wurde beispielsweise von den Vereinten Nationen zur „Designhauptstadt" erklärt. Viele Aktivitäten werden nun durch Staatsgelder unterstützt, wobei Fachleute direkt in die Entscheidungsprozesse der städtischen Entwicklung eingebunden werden.

Nachdem die Verpackungsbranche in China all diese Phasen durchlaufen hat, haben wir allen Grund zu der Annahme, dass sie sich sehr positiven Zukunftsaussichten gegenübersieht und eine wichtige Rolle in der Globalisierung der Wirtschaft spielen wird. Im Zuge dieser Entwicklung wird China sicherlich noch viele ausgezeichnete Designer hervorbringen, die das Rückgrat der Branche bilden werden. In diesem Buch präsentieren wir eine Anzahl anschaulicher Projekte, die zeigen, wie chinesische Designer mit ihren Auftraggebern und Kunden kommunizieren und ihre Ideen auf den Markt ausweiten.

dans le domaine du design, en élaborant des règles pour que l'industrie se développe rapidement et en fixant des objectifs. Par exemple, la ville de Shenzhen a été déclarée « capitale du design » par les Nations Unies, et de nombreuses activités de design reçoivent désormais des aides gouvernementales, des professionnels étant directement impliqués dans la prise de décisions en matière de développement urbain.

Sachant que l'industrie du design d'emballages en Chine est passée par toutes ces phases, nous avons des raisons de croire qu'elle a devant elle un horizon très positif et qu'elle jouera un rôle important dans la globalisation de l'économie. Au cours de ce processus de développement, nombre d'excellents designers en Chine se placeront comme le pivot de l'industrie. Nous présentons dans cet ouvrage plusieurs projets brillants qui montrent comment les designers chinois communiquent avec leurs clients et leur public, et comment ils projettent leurs idées sur le marché.

Japanese Graphic Design

by Sadao Maekawa

Marcos Sadao Maekawa was born in São Paulo and after graduating in Architecture and Urbanism at university he moved to Japan to work as a graphic and editorial designer for Japanese and foreign design, publishing, and advertising companies in Tokyo. After 12 years in the printing field, Maekawa took a Masters degree in Media Design and is now in the PhD programme at Keio University. He also works as a freelance writer/designer and is a big fan of Asian food, Japanese pop music, and gadgets.

Marcos Sadao Maekawa wurde in São Paulo geboren. Nach dem Abschluss seines Architektur- und Städtebaustudiums ging er nach Japan, um in Tokio als redaktioneller und Grafikdesigner für in- und ausländische Design-, Verlags- und Werbeunternehmen zu arbeiten. Nach zwölfjähriger Tätigkeit im Printbereich promoviert Maekawa derzeit an der Keio-Universität im Fachbereich Mediendesign. Darüber hinaus ist der große Fan von asiatischem Essen, japanischer Popmusik und elektronischen Gadgets freiberuflich als Autor und Designer tätig.

Marcos Sadao Maekawa est né à São Paulo. Après ses études universitaires d'architecture et d'urbanisme, il s'est installé au Japon pour exercer en tant que designer graphique et éditorial pour des agences de design, de publication et de publicité du Japon et étrangères se trouvant à Tokyo. Après 12 ans dans le secteur de l'impression, Maekawa a passé un master de design multimédia et prépare actuellement un doctorat à l'université de Keio. Il travaille aussi souvent comme écrivain/designer freelance et est un inconditionnel de cuisine asiatique, de musique pop japonaise et de gadgets.

The boom in Japanese graphic design began in the second half of the 20th Century and became a benchmark, not just for Asia – where it gained many converts – but worldwide. After the end of World War II, Japan launched an aggressive campaign of cultural exchange in a bid to regain its former position in international society. The government drew up plans to spread Japanese culture to other parts of the world and, at the same time, to introduce Western culture into everyday life in Japan. One result of these endeavours came in 1964, when Tokyo hosted the Olympic Games. This opened a new chapter in the country's contemporary history, showing the world its expertise in technology – and graphic design.

Der Boom des japanischen Grafikdesigns begann in der zweiten Hälfte des 20. Jahrhunderts und wurde zum Maßstab – nicht nur in Asien, wo sich viele bekehren ließen, sondern weltweit. Nach Ende des Zweiten Weltkriegs startete Japan in dem Bestreben, seine frühere Position in der internationalen Gesellschaft wiederzuerlangen, eine aggressive Kampagne des kulturellen Austauschs. Die Regierung erstellte Pläne, um die japanische Kultur in andere Gegenden der Welt zu exportieren und gleichzeitig die westliche Kultur in das japanische Alltagsleben einzuführen. Als ein Ergebnis dieser Bemühungen wurde Tokio 1964 zum Gastgeber der Olympischen Sommerspiele. Damit wurde ein neues Kapitel in der jüngeren japanischen Geschichte aufgeschlagen: Das Land führte

Le boom du design graphique japonais a commencé dans la seconde moitié du XXe siècle et est devenu une référence faisant de nombreux adeptes en Asie, mais aussi dans le monde entier. Au terme de la Seconde Guerre mondiale, le Japon a lancé une campagne agressive d'échanges culturels en vue de reconquérir sa position antérieure dans la société internationale. Le gouvernement a élaboré des plans pour diffuser la culture japonaise à d'autres parties du monde, tout en introduisant en parallèle la culture occidentale dans la vie quotidienne du pays. En 1964 s'appréciait un résultat de ces efforts avec l'organisation des Jeux olympiques à Tokyo. Cet événement a ouvert un nouveau chapitre dans l'histoire contemporaine du pays, prouvant au monde ses compétences

ma-pattern
poster, by Sayaco Takasaki,
Japan

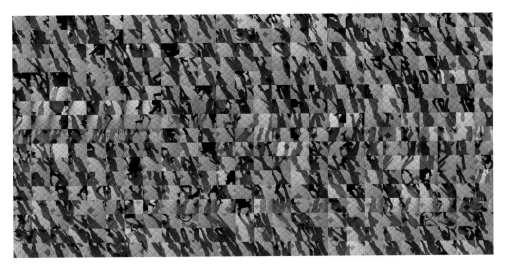

This event was a major milestone for Japanese graphic design. Yusaku Kamekura charmed the world with his posters for the Tokyo Olympics. The art director Masaru Katsumi headed the development of the signage system, introducing pictograms to represent each type of Olympic sport. The visual language, still in use today, was devised to help communicate with visitors to the first Olympics ever staged in Asia. It was in the same period – the '50s and '60s – that Japanese design really took off. The movement led by Katsumi created specialist schools of design and arts education centres for school-age children, as well as setting up "good design corners" in big department stores, all with the aim of educating the population about good design.

The years that followed were marked by Japanese style icons like Ikko Tanaka, Kazumasa Nagai, and Shigeo Fukuda, with their posters and audacious graphics. Japan's high-quality printing technology also helped publicise Japanese design on the international stage, combining as it did traditional and contemporary, East and West, to create its own unique and unmistakable identity.

Efforts to promote design to Japanese society have borne fruit, and public awareness of design is impressive. Design is so

der Welt seine Kompetenz in Sachen Technologie und Grafikdesign vor Augen.

Dieses Ereignis war ein bedeutender Meilenstein für Japans Grafikdesign. Yusaku Kamekura bezauberte die Welt mit seinen Plakaten für die Olympiade in Tokio. Masaru Katsumi leitete als Art Director die Entwicklung des Beschilderungssystems, das Piktogramme einführte, die die verschiedenen olympischen Sportdisziplinen repräsentierten. Die auch heute noch verwendete visuelle Sprache wurde entwickelt, um mit den Besuchern der ersten Olympiade zu kommunizieren, die jemals in Asien stattfand. In eben dieser Periode – also in den 1950er- und 60er-Jahren – startete das japanische Design regelrecht durch. Die von Katsumi geführte Bewegung begründete auf Design spezialisierte Schulen sowie Kunst-Ausbildungsstätten für Kinder im Schulalter und richtete „Bereiche mit vorbildlichem Design" in großen Kaufhäusern ein – alles mit dem Ziel, die Bevölkerung in Bezug auf gutes Design zu schulen.

Die folgenden Jahre waren von japanischen Stilikonen wie Ikko Tanaka, Kazumasa Nagai und Shigeo Fukuda mit ihren Plakaten und kühnen Grafiken gekennzeichnet. Die qualitativ hochwertige Drucktechnik Japans trug ebenfalls dazu bei, japanisches Design auf der internationalen Bühne zu präsen-

en matière de technologie et de design graphique.

Les J.O. ont en effet été déterminants pour le design graphique japonais, et Yusaku Kamekura a conquis le monde avec les affiches créées pour cette occasion. Le directeur artistique Masaru s'est chargé de concevoir le système de signalisation, en intégrant des pictogrammes pour symboliser chaque discipline olympique. Encore d'actualité, le langage visuel a été pensé pour communiquer avec les visiteurs de ces premières olympiades organisées en Asie. C'est pendant cette même période, des années 50 et 60, que le design japonais a vraiment décollé. Le mouvement conduit par Katsumi a créé des écoles spécialisées de design et des centres d'enseignement artistique pour les enfants d'âge scolaire. Il a aussi installé des « stands de design de qualité » dans les grands magasins, afin de former la population au bon design.

Des icônes du style japonais, comme Ikko Tanaka, Kazumasa Nagai et Shigeo Fukuda, ont marqué les années suivantes avec leurs affiches et leurs graphismes audacieux. La technologie d'impression de haute qualité a aussi contribué à diffuser le design nippon sur la scène internationale, en combinant le traditionnel et le contemporain, l'Est et l'Ouest, origine de son identité unique et indubitable.

TO KYO TO
poster, 2006, by Shinnoske
Sugisaki, Shinnoske
Design Inc., AGI (Alliance
Graphique Internationale),
Japan

Fishing Net
poster campaign, 1998,
by Norito Shinmura,
Shinmura Design Office,
Shinmura Fisheries,
Japan

much a part of everyday life in Japan that you are just as likely to come across it on Hokkaido, the island in the extreme north, or in the province of Fukuoka in the south of the archipelago, as in the capital, Tokyo. There are countless vocational schools, degree courses, design studios, and agencies scattered across the country. Logos, packaging, mascots, adverts, publications, and publicity in general are available to the public and are by no means synonymous with luxury. The dream of making design accessible to everyone has been realised.

The penetration of design into society at large has created an eclecticism seldom seen in other countries. Traditional elements are mixed with daring, modern graphics. Clean, almost minimalist, design contrasts with organised chaos. Monochrome appears as often as bright, vibrant colours. But, most interestingly, this eclecticism is born out of a hybrid culture that displays a level of sophistication, sensitivity, and cohesion, a combination difficult to find in graphic, industrial, digital, or architectural design anywhere else in the world.

These contrasts are no more than a reflection of all the transformations that Japanese society itself underwent in the second half of the 20th Century. And what must be one of the most hackneyed

tieren, indem sie Traditionelles und Zeitgenössisches, Östliches und Westliches zu einer einzigartigen und unverwechselbaren Identität verband.

Die Bestrebungen, das Design in der japanischen Gesellschaft zu fördern, trugen Früchte, und das öffentliche Design-Bewusstsein ist beeindruckend. Design ist so stark in das japanische Alltagsleben integriert, dass man es auf der im äußersten Norden gelegenen Insel Hokkaido ebenso selbstverständlich antrifft wie in der Provinz Fukuoka im Süden des Archipels und in der Hauptstadt Tokio. Es gibt zahllose Berufsschulen, Studiengänge, Designstudios und Agenturen, die über das ganze Land verstreut sind. Logos, Verpackung, Maskottchen, Werbung, Publikationen und Reklame generell stehen für die Öffentlichkeit bereit und sind beileibe kein Synonym für Luxus. Der Traum davon, Design für alle zugänglich zu machen, ist Wirklichkeit geworden.

Die Durchdringung der gesamten Gesellschaft mit Design führte zu einem Eklektizismus, der in anderen Ländern seinesgleichen sucht. Traditionelle Elemente werden mit gewagten, modernen Grafiken vermischt. Klares, geradezu minimalistisches Design kontrastiert mit dem organisierten Chaos. Monochromes steht gleichberechtigt neben leuchtenden, lebendigen Farben. Doch am

Les efforts de promotion du design auprès de la société japonaise ont porté leurs fruits ; la sensibilité du public envers le design est d'ailleurs impressionnante. Le design fait tellement partie intégrante du quotidien au Japon que vous pouvez autant en trouver des exemples sur l'île d'Hokkaido à l'extrême nord, dans la province de Fukuoka au sud de l'archipel, que dans la capitale. D'innombrables écoles professionnelles, cursus universitaires, studios de design et agences sont répartis sur tout le territoire. Logos, emballages, mascottes, annonces, publications et publicité sont en général disponibles pour le public et n'ont rien d'un luxe. Le rêve de rendre le design accessible à tous s'est matérialisé.

La pénétration à grande échelle du design dans la société a créé un éclecticisme rare dans d'autres pays. Les aspects traditionnels se marient à des graphismes modernes et osés ; un design propre, presque minimaliste, contraste avec le chaos organisé ; le monochrome est aussi fréquent que les couleurs vives. Le mieux est que cet éclecticisme est né d'une culture hybride, forte d'un niveau de sophistication, de sensibilité et de cohésion, un mariage difficile à trouver ailleurs dans le domaine du design graphique, industriel, numérique ou architectural.

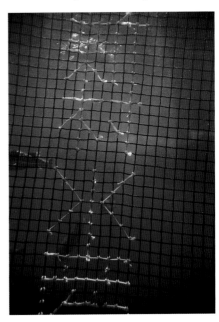

clichés used to describe a country where "the modern and the traditional and other contrasts live together in complete harmony" can also be applied to the country's graphic design. Living in Japan means that, wherever you happen to be, you are constantly surrounded by design and other visual references. The current scenario is a legacy of Japan's traditional culture, one deeply influenced by ideograms, landscapes, and clearly-defined seasons of the year, as well as by cuisine, fashions, make-up, and Japanese arts in general.

The last years of the first decade of the 21st Century brought changes that were bound to impact on the future of graphic design. Technological innovations, such as advanced software, more powerful computers, and changes in the way people work and communicate with each other, helped creative artists to go beyond the boundaries. Meanwhile, the Internet opened up fresh possibilities in every sector, also enabling the digital world to be extended to people right across the planet.

At present, Japan, like the rest of the world, is going through a delicate phase, and some have dared to say that the days of graphic design and print media are numbered. Recently, Dentsu, the country's largest advertising agency, revealed that, in

interessantesten ist, dass dieser Eklektizismus aus einer hybriden Kultur geboren wurde, die ein Maß an Raffinesse, Feinfühligkeit und Zusammengehörigkeit aufweist, wie man es im Grafik- und Industriedesign, in den digitalen Medien oder in der Architektur anderswo auf der Erde nur schwerlich findet.

Diese Kontraste reflektieren lediglich all jene Umgestaltungen, denen sich die japanische Gesellschaft in der zweiten Hälfte des 20. Jahrhunderts unterziehen musste. Und was man als eines der abgedroschensten Klischees bezeichnen muss, mit dem man ein Land beschreiben kann, in dem „das Moderne und das Traditionelle und andere Kontraste in vollendeter Harmonie zusammenleben", gilt auch für das Grafikdesign des Landes: In Japan zu leben bedeutet, ständig von Design und anderen visuellen Referenzen umgeben zu sein – egal, wo man sich gerade aufhält. Das gegenwärtige Szenario ist das Erbe der traditionellen japanischen Kultur, die tief von Ideogrammen, Landschaften und klar voneinander abgegrenzten Jahreszeiten beeinflusst wird – ebenso wie von der landeseigenen Küche, der Mode, dem Make-up und der japanischen Kunst generell.

Die letzten Jahre des ersten Jahrzehnts im 21. Jahrhundert brachten Veränderungen, die sich auch auf die Zukunft des Grafikdesigns auswirken werden. Techno-

Ces contrastes sont le simple reflet de toutes les transformations vécues par la propre société nippone au cours de la seconde moitié du XXe siècle. Ce qui est sans doute l'un des clichés le plus rebattus pour décrire un pays où « le moderne et la tradition et d'autres contrastes cohabitent en totale harmonie » peut aussi s'appliquer au design graphique du pays. Vivre n'importe où au Japon signifie être constamment entouré de design et d'autres références visuelles. Le scénario actuel est un héritage de la culture traditionnelle du Japon, profondément influencée par des idéogrammes, des paysages et des saisons très marquées, ainsi que par la gastronomie, la mode, le maquillage et l'art nippon en général.

Les dernières années de la première décennie du XXIe siècle ont apporté des changements qui auront forcément un impact sur l'avenir du design graphique. Les innovations technologiques, comme les logiciels sophistiqués, les ordinateurs plus puissants et l'évolution des modes de travail et de communication ont permis aux artistes de dépasser les limites. En parallèle, Internet a ouvert des portes dans chaque secteur, permettant à l'univers numérique de parvenir aux personnes à travers toute la planète.

Aujourd'hui, le Japon, comme le reste du monde, traverse un moment délicat ;

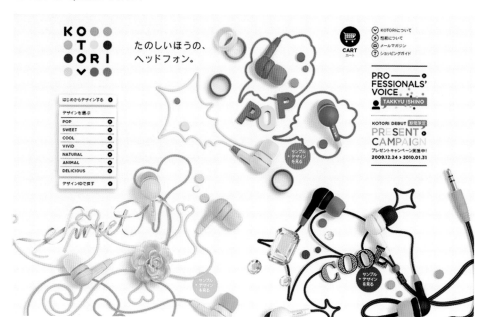

Kotori
website, 2009,
by IMG SRC,
Japan

2009, expenditure on advertising in Japan suffered the sharpest drop in its history. Investments in print media, where once the figures were astronomical, are losing out to investments in digital media, which for the first time overtook spending on newspaper advertising and now occupy second place in the field, behind TV. But despite these upheavals, Japanese graphic design still has plenty of room for innovation.

Japan is a country where design rather than price is what sells the product, a place where packaging made for *natto* (fermented soya beans) bears the signature of a famous designer while *sushi* is cleverly used in the campaign to launch a new fashion collection. Seemingly, the economic downturn is having no effect on Japanese graphic design. Quite the opposite – the crisis is just one more challenge facing the country's designers, who are continuing to search for new solutions to make life more comfortable, more informative, and more interesting for their fellow citizens. Daily existence is still full of visual references and Japan's traditional technical prowess and perfectionism serve as a legacy to inspire what is currently being produced by digital media and design – but these are the subject of another book. Japan, once famous for exporting technol-

logische Innovationen wie z. B. hochentwickelte Software, leistungsfähigere Computer und die veränderte Weise, wie Menschen miteinander arbeiten und kommunizieren, haben kreativen Künstlern dazu verholfen, Grenzen zu überschreiten. Inzwischen hat das Internet in jedem Bereich neue, unverbrauchte Möglichkeiten eröffnet und es der digitalen Welt ermöglicht, Menschen auf der ganzen Welt zu erreichen.

Derzeit durchläuft Japan wie auch die restliche Welt eine heikle Phase, und mancher wagt gar zu behaupten, die Tage des Grafikdesigns und der Printmedien seien gezählt. Kürzlich meldete Dentsu, Japans größte Werbeagentur, dass die Werbeausgaben im Jahre 2009 den tiefsten Sturz ihrer Geschichte erlitten haben. Die Investitionen in Printmedien, wo die Umsatzzahlen früher einmal astronomisch zu nennen waren, gehen im Vergleich zu denen in digitale Medien zurück, die zum ersten Mal die Ausgaben für Zeitungswerbung überholten und nun nach dem Fernsehen in diesem Bereich den zweiten Platz einnehmen. Doch trotz dieser Umbrüche verfügt das japanische Grafikdesign immer noch über sehr viel Raum für Innovationen.

Japan ist ein Land, in dem Produkte sich eher über ihre Gestaltung als über ihren Preis verkaufen, ein Ort, in dem eine für Natto (fermentierte Sojabohnen) gefertigte

certains augurent même que les jours sont comptés pour le design graphique et les travaux d'impression. Récemment Dentsu, la plus importante agence de publicité du pays, a révélé que le Japon avait enregistré en 2009 la baisse la plus importante de son histoire en dépenses publicitaires. Les investissements dans les publications, avec des chiffres auparavant astronomiques, cèdent du terrain à ceux dans les supports numériques : pour la première fois, ces derniers ont dépassé les journaux en matière de dépenses de publicité et occupent la deuxième place derrière la télévision. Malgré ces bouleversements, le design graphique japonais garde encore plein de marge pour l'innovation.

Le Japon est un pays où les produits se vendent plus par rapport au design qu'à leur prix, où les emballages fabriqués à base de *natto* (graines de soja fermentées) portent la signature d'un célèbre designer, alors que les *sushi* sont intelligemment utilisés dans une campagne pour lancer une nouvelle collection de vêtements. De la même façon, la baisse économique est sans incidence sur le design graphique japonais, au contraire : la crise représente un défi de plus pour les designers du pays, toujours en quête de nouvelles solutions pour rendre la vie de la population plus agréable, plus instructive

Mount Fuji
The Poster Exhibition
Inspired by Hokusai's 36
Views of Mount Fuji, 2007,
by U.G. Sato, JAGDA,
Japan

ogy, now exports "soft" power, in other
words, its traditional and pop cultures,
in which graphic design plays a leading
role. *Asian Graphics Now!* looks at cutting-
edge developments in Japan and in neigh-
bouring countries in Asia. *Otanoshimini!*
(Enjoy!)

Verpackung die Signatur eines berühmten
Designers trägt, während *sushi* auf pfiffige
Weise bei einer Kampagne verwendet wird,
um eine neue Modekollektion vorzustellen.
Offenbar wirkt sich der ökonomische Ab-
schwung nicht auf das japanische Grafikdesign aus. Ganz im Gegenteil: Die Krise ist
nur eine weitere Herausforderung, der sich
die Designer des Landes stellen, die weiter-
hin nach neuen Lösungen suchen, um das
Leben für ihre Mitbürger angenehmer, infor-
mativer und interessanter zu machen. Das
Alltagsleben ist immer noch voller visueller
Referenzen, und Japans traditionelles tech-
nisches Können sowie sein Perfektionismus
dienen als Erbe, um das zu inspirieren, was
mittels digitaler Medien und Design aktuell
produziert wird – aber das ist das Thema
eines anderen Buches. Japan war einmal
berühmt dafür, Technologie zu exportieren,
und exportiert nun seine „weichen" Kräfte –
anders gesagt: seine traditionelle und seine
populäre Kultur, in der das Grafikdesign eine
führende Rolle spielt. *Asian Graphics Now!*
wirft einen Blick auf die aktuellsten Entwicklungen in Japan und bei seinen asiatischen
Nachbarn. *Otanoshimini!* (Viel Spaß!)

et plus intéressante. Le quotidien est rem-
pli de références visuelles, et la prouesse
et le perfectionnisme traditionnels servent
d'inspirations aux créations actuelles pour
les supports et le design numériques (un
sujet pour un autre ouvrage). D'abord célèbre exportateur de technologie, le Japon
exporte maintenant une force « artistique »,
en d'autres termes ses cultures traditionnel-
les et populaires dans lesquelles le design
graphique joue un rôle clé. *Asian Graphics
Now!* se penche sur les œuvres d'avant-garde au Japon et dans les pays voisins d'Asie.
Otanoshimini! (Amusez-vous bien!)

They

advertising + poster

PROJECT
JAGDA Graphic Design
in Japan, *posters*,
JAGDA

COUNTRY
Japan

YEAR
2009

DESIGN
10 Inc.

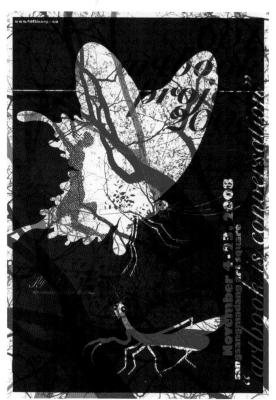

PROJECT

601Artbook Project
Exhibition, *posters*,
KT&G SangSangMadand
Art Market

COUNTRY

South Korea

YEAR

2008

DESIGN

601bisang

TEAM

Kum-jun Park

PROJECT
601Artbook Project
Exhibition, *posters*,
KT&G SangSangMadand
Art Market

COUNTRY
South Korea

YEAR
2009

DESIGN
601bisang

TEAM
Kum-jun Park

PROJECT
601Artbook Project
Exhibition, *posters*,
KT&G SangSangMadand
Art Market

DESIGN
601bisang

TEAM
Kum-jun Park

COUNTRY
South Korea

YEAR
2007

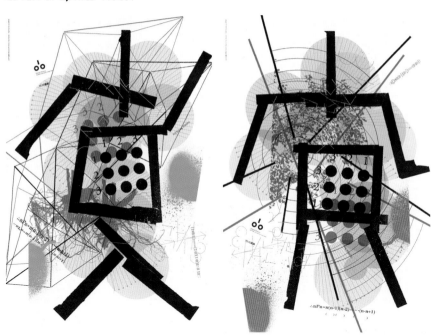

PROJECT
Visual Poetry, *posters*,
Mankind (The bearer of
the Universe)

COUNTRY
South Korea

YEAR
2010

DESIGN
601bisang

TEAM
Kum-jun Park

BALLERINA WHO LOVES B-BOYZ

project
Ballerina who loves B-boyz,
posters, B-boyz Theatre

country
South Korea

year
2005

design
601bisang

team
Kum-jun Park

BLESS CHINA·
COMMEMORATION
OF
5.12
CHINA'S
MASSIVE
EARTHQUAKE

PROJECT

Bless China,
Commemoration of
China's Earthquake, *poster*,
personal work

COUNTRY

South Korea

YEAR

2009

DESIGN

601bisang

TEAM

Kum-jun Park

PROJECT

Love & Peace, *posters*,
Personal work

COUNTRY

South Korea

YEAR

2009

DESIGN

601bisang

TEAM

Kum-jun Park

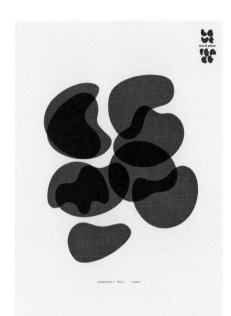

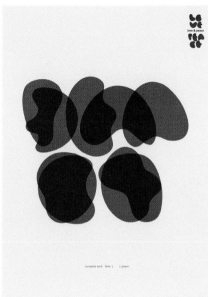

project
NHK Kodomo, *poster*,
NHK National Television

country
Japan

year
2009

design
10 Inc.

www.nhk.or.jp/heart-net/kodomo/

PROJECT
"Chen Sinjin" and
"Oh Wen Xin", posters

COUNTRY
Japan

YEAR
2009

DESIGN
Akio Okumura

PROJECT
Picasso de Sakaso, poster,
Tokushima Modern Art
Museum

COUNTRY
Japan

YEAR
2009

DESIGN
Akio Okumura

徳島県立近代美術館　デザインプロジェクト

ピカソ
de
さがそ!

PICASSO × De FESTA 2009

The Tokushima Modern Art Museum Design Project

project
Science Visualization
Society of Japan, *posters*

country
Japan

year
2009

design
Akio Okumura

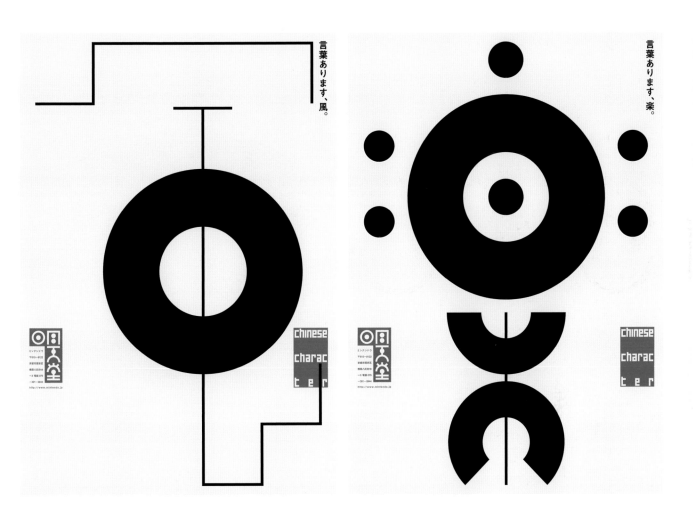

project

There is a word, *posters*,
Mintendo Co., Ltd.

country

Japan

year

2008

design

Akio Okumura

FUTURE ACADEMIC 1

**2008
07.29.tue
open**

**2008
08.03.sun
close**

*We dig for the unknown,
reveal fact, and let shine
the bright light at
the center of each being.*

DIC! DIC!

BRI GHT!

**ALLRAID
GRAPHICS**
-Graphic Design-

**MASATO
YAMAGUCHI**
-Painting-

PROLOGUE

The freedom of producing an original academic art movement results in a driving force of innovative young ideas, wonderful dreams and open hearts and the creation of novel yet disciplined artwork. Since the establishment of Future Academic in 2008 these are the ideas that have propelled our efforts. As industry, art, economics, and manufacturing come to a great crossroads, we're carving a new future based on ideas that spread from the Antarctic to the Arabian deserts, traversing the equator and reaching the frozen North. With our recently discovered truth detecting device we've found a body of 28 artists, musicians, DJs, graphic designers, architects, authors, editors, and cultural creators. This inaugural "FUTURE ACADEMIC 1" will showcase works from ALLRAID GRAPHICS, Rie Shimizu, Hitoyo Karino, and Masato Yamaguchi.

**RIE
SHIMIZU**
-Oil Painting-

**HITOYO
KARINO**
-PROPAGANDA-

ACCESS

11:00

19:00

CASPER'S GALLERY
〒153-0042 1-25-4 Aobadai Meguro-ku Tokyo
Telephone:03-6806-1671/Facsimile:03-6806-1672/www.caspers-g.com

BOSTEX

ALLRAID GRAPHICS

project
Future Academic, *posters*,
Allraid Graphics

country
Japan

year
2008

design
Allraid Graphics

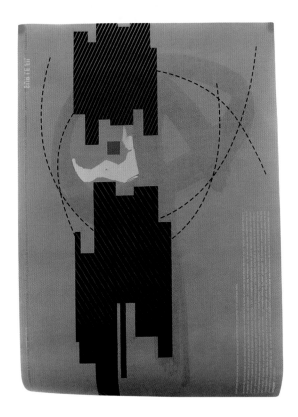

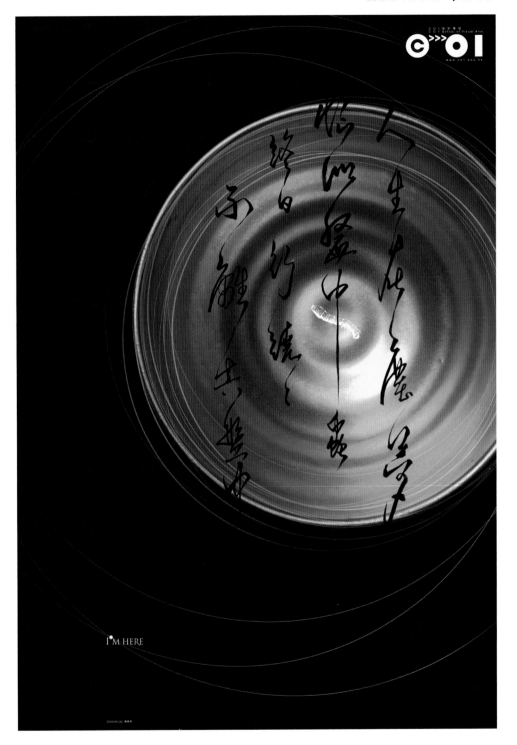

project
Sur le fil, *posters*, French
Ministry of Foreign Affairs
and Culturesfra

country
China

year
2007

design
Chen Zhengda

team
Chen Zhengda,
Carla Talopp (France)

project
I'm here Exhibition, *poster*,
CO1 Design School

country
Hong Kong/China

year
2007

design
Ameba Design

team
Gideon Lai, Kenji

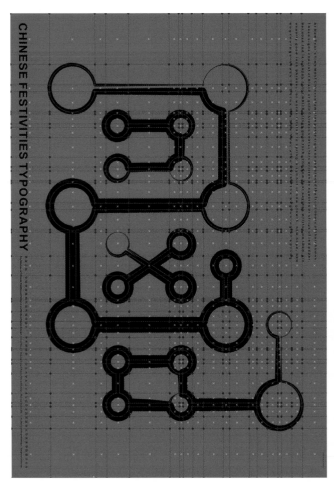

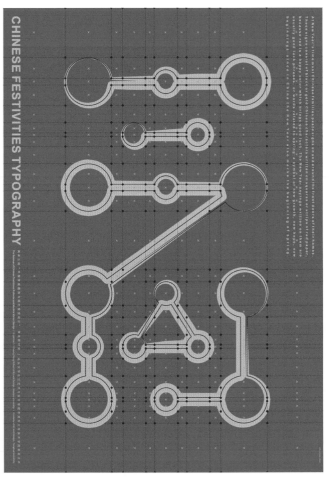

PROJECT
Chinese Festivities
Typography, *posters*,
Academy of Arts & Design
of Tsinghua University

COUNTRY
China

YEAR
2004

DESIGN
Chen Zhengda

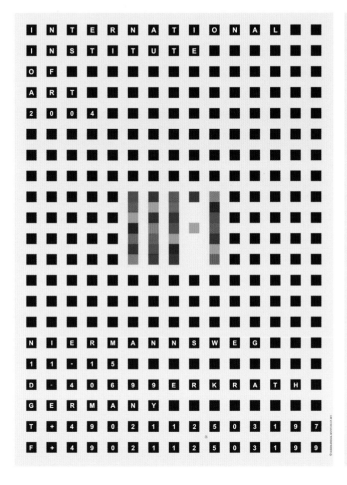
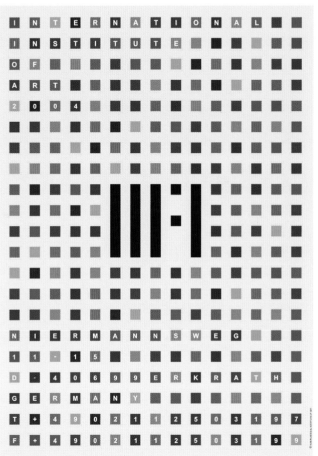

project
International Institute
of Art (IIA), *logo design
and posters*

country
China

year
2004

design
Chen Zhengda

PROJECT
Here Lies the Body of
My Poster, *posters*,
California Institute
of the Arts

COUNTRY
South Korea

YEAR
2006

DESIGN
Jiwon Lee

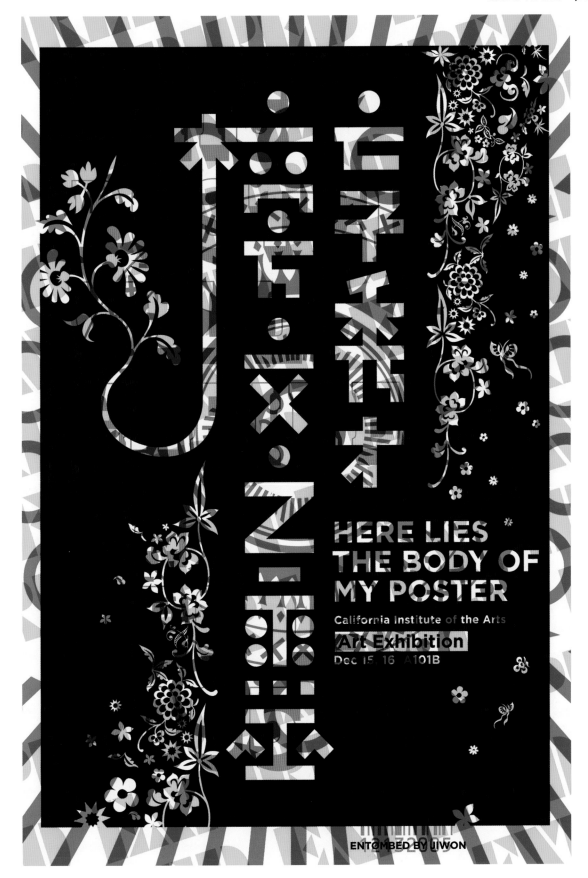

HERE LIES
THE BODY OF
MY POSTER

California Institute of the Arts

Art Exhibition
Dec 15, 16 A101B

ENTOMBED BY JIWON

PROJECT

Graduation Festivity,
poster, California Institute
of the Arts

COUNTRY

China

YEAR

2006

DESIGN

Jiwon Lee, Hazeline Ko

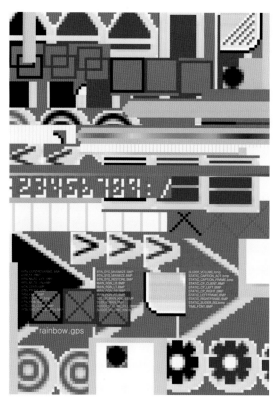

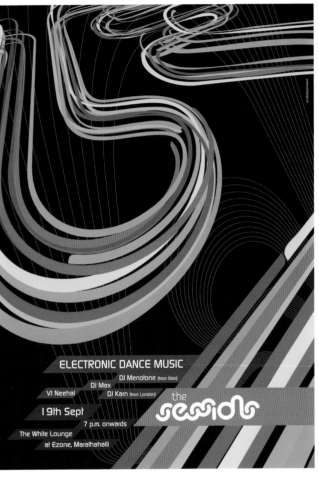

11. SEP. 2001
THE 9.11 ATTACKS TO WTC
PRE ORGANIC COTTON×DESIGN
T-SHIRTS PROJECT BY KURKKU

26 APR 1986
THE CHERNOBYL DISASTER
PRE ORGANIC COTTON×DESIGN
T-SHIRTS PROJECT BY KURKKU

9 NOV 1989
THE FALL OF BERLIN WALL
PRE ORGANIC COTTON×DESIGN
T-SHIRTS PROJECT BY KURKKU

4. OCT. 1957
SPUTNIK 1 WAS LAUNCHED
PRE ORGANIC COTTON×DESIGN
T-SHIRTS PROJECT BY KURKKU

20. 7. 1969
THE 1ST STEP ON THE MOON
PRE ORGANIC COTTON×DESIGN
T-SHIRTS PROJECT BY KURKKU

Project
Pre Organic Cotton,
Design T-Shirts Project,
posters, Kurkku

Country
Japan

Year
2009

Design
Good Design Company

Team
Art Direction:
Mizuno Manabu
Design:
Kunou Mari

Project
Salon Christmas, *greeting
card and posters*, Salon

Country
Japan

Year
2009

Design
Good Design Company

Team
Art Direction:
Mizuno Manabu
Design:
Kunou Mari

MERRY X'MAS

AND A HAPPY NEW YEAR!

Happy holidays! This year went so fast. I hope
It was a good one and the next even better.

2009-10

Jingle bells! Jingle bells! Jingle all the way!
Oh, what fun it is to ride in a one-horse open sleigh!

Salon

DE BEERS GINZA BUILDING 5F, 2.5.11, GINZA, CHUO-KU, TOKYO JAPAN

ZIP 104.0061

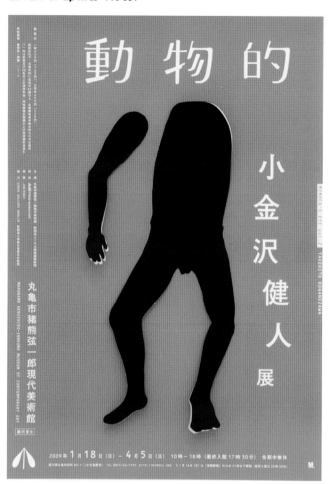

PROJECT
Mimoca's Eye Vol. 2,
Takehito Koganezawa,
poster, Marugame
Genichiro-Inokuma
Museum of
Contemporary Art

COUNTRY
Japan

YEAR
2009

DESIGN
Bluemark Inc.

TEAM
Art Direction/Design:
Atsuki Kikuchi
Illustration:
Takehito Koganezawa
Printing Director:
Takashi Ochiai

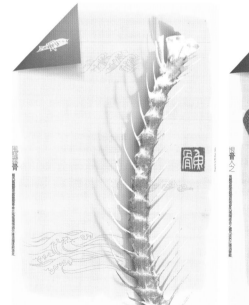

PROJECT
National Standard 2005
S/S, *poster*, National
Standard

COUNTRY
Japan

YEAR
2005

DESIGN
Bluemark Inc.

TEAM
Art Direction/Design:
Atsuki Kikuchi
Illustration:
Yusuke Saito,
Asami Hattori
Printing Director:
Takashi Ochiai

PROJECT
Mimoca's Eye Vol. 2,
Takehito Koganezawa,
posters, Marugame
Genichiro-Inokuma
Museum of
Contemporary Art

COUNTRY
Japan

YEAR
2009

DESIGN
Bluemark Inc.

TEAM
Art Direction/Design:
Atsuki Kikuchi
Illustration:
Takehito Koganezawa
Printing Director:
Takashi Ochiai

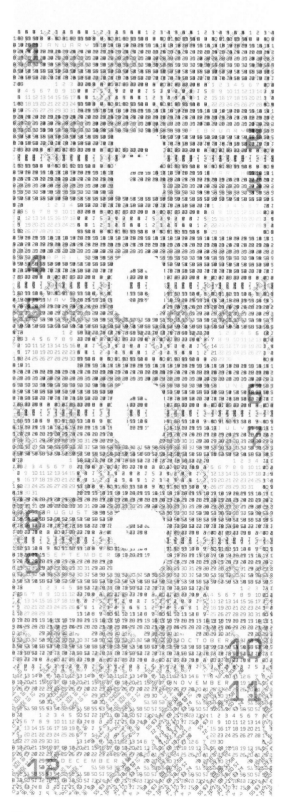

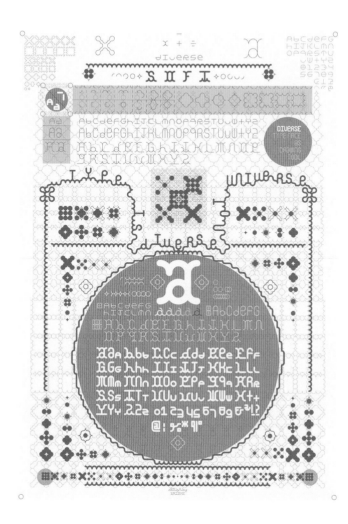

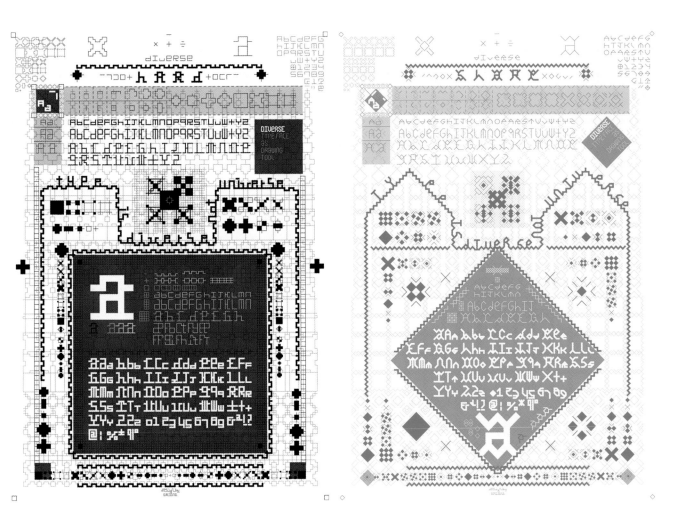

PROJECT
Typeface as Drawing Tool,
posters

COUNTRY
South Korea

YEAR
2009

DESIGN
Goo-Ryong Kang

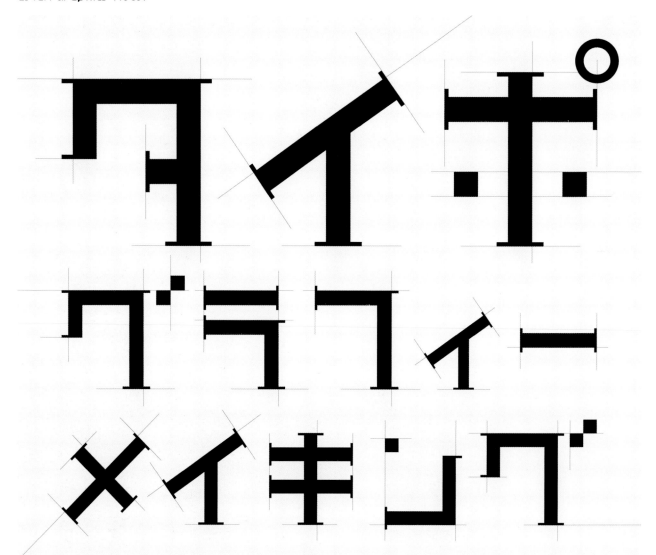

Typography
Making

38pt/45pt
Monotype Baskerville

Applications

SEIBUNDO
SHINKOSHA

Logomark:
Cyan90%+Magenta50%

Logotype:
Black70%

タイポグラフィーの現場 12pt

味岡伸太郎／佐野研二郎／甲谷一 20pt

本明朝BOOK 新がな + Monotype Baskerville

丸明オールド組み版の原点に還る。

片岡朗

雑誌・書籍のタイトルロゴの世界

ベター・デイズ　大久保裕文

Illustrator & Photoshopで作るロゴ、

タイポグラフィーのメイキング満載

PROJECT

Typography Making,
poster, Seibundo
Shinkosha

COUNTRY

Japan

YEAR

2009

DESIGN

Happy & Happy

TEAM

Hajime Kabutoya

PROJECT

The European Art Market,
poster, China Academy
of Art

COUNTRY

China

YEAR

2004

DESIGN

Chen Zhengda

PROJECT
Time, *poster*,
personal work

COUNTRY
South Korea

YEAR
2009

DESIGN
Heesun Seo

PROJECT
4:30, *posters*, Royston Tan

COUNTRY
Singapore

YEAR
2006

DESIGN
&Larry

TEAM
Creative Director/Designer:
Larry Peh

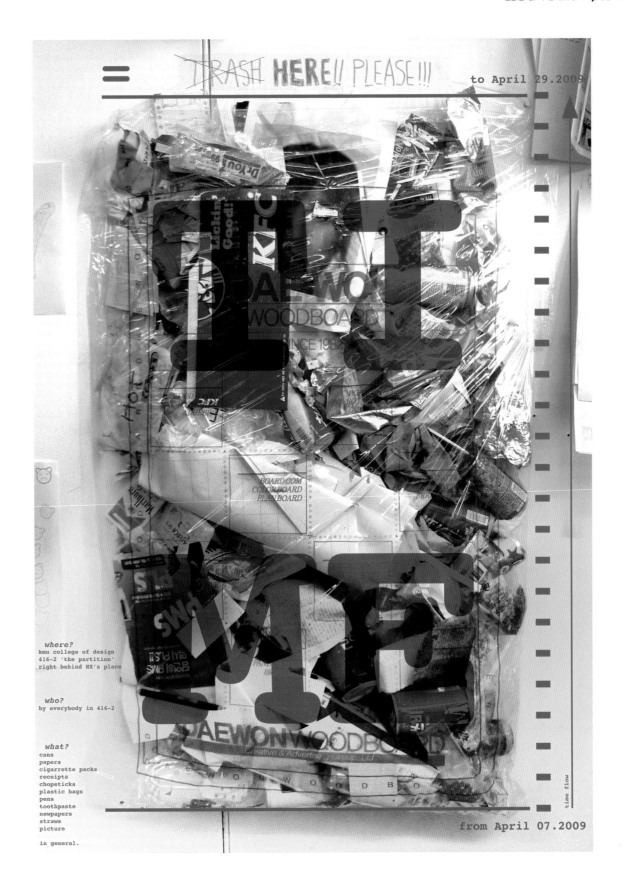

PROJECT
Nico, *posters*

COUNTRY
Japan

YEAR
2009

DESIGN
MR_DESIGN

TEAM
Art Director:
Kenjiro Sano,
Designer:
Masashi Murakami

PROJECT
Love Distance, *online
campaign*, Sagami Rubber
Industries

COUNTRY
Japan

YEAR
2009

DESIGN
NON-GRID,
IMG SRC Group

TEAM
Naoki Ito, Masaki Endo,
Qanta Shimizu, Atsuki
Yukawa, Kenichi Takahashi,
Hiroaki Kitamura,
Hiroki Hara, Yukihiro
Sasae, Mio Yamashita,
Atsushi Fujimaki,
Takeshi Yoshimori, Saiko
Kamikanda, Jun Koriyama,
Takuho Yoshizu, Masanori
Mori, rhizomatiks

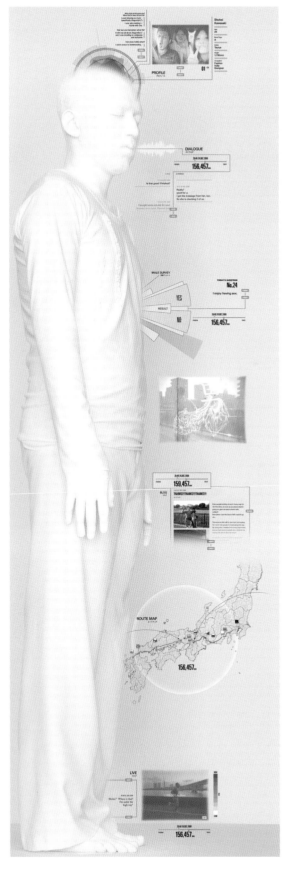

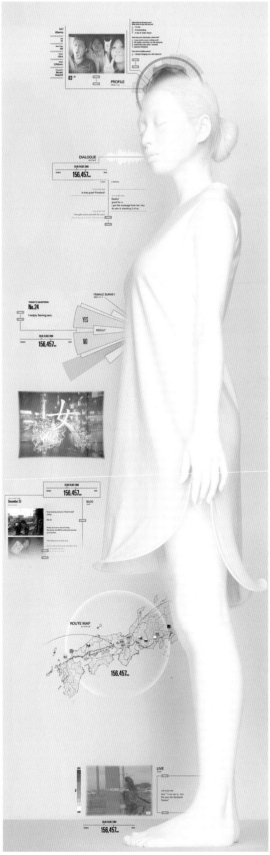

Laforet Private Party

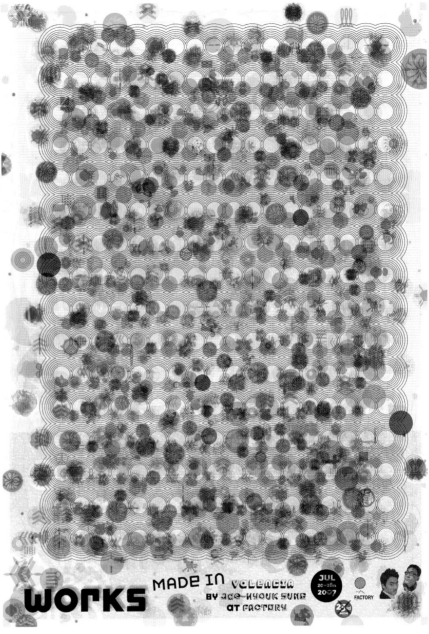

PROJECT
Laforet Private Party,
poster, Laforet

COUNTRY
Japan

YEAR
2008

DESIGN
Good Design Company

TEAM
Mizuno Manabu

PROJECT
Works Made in Valencia,
posters, personal work

COUNTRY
South Korea

YEAR
2007

DESIGN
Jae-Hyouk Sung

TEAM
Jae-Hyouk Sung,
Minsun Eo,
Goo-Ryong Kang

PROJECT
Magnum Autumn/Winter,
poster, Art Tower Mito

COUNTRY
Japan

YEAR
2005

DESIGN
FLAME Inc.

TEAM
Masayoshi Kodaira

PROJECT
Archigram: experimental
architecture 1961–1974,
Poster, Art Tower Mito

COUNTRY
Japan

YEAR
2005

DESIGN
FLAME Inc.

TEAM
Masayoshi Kodaira

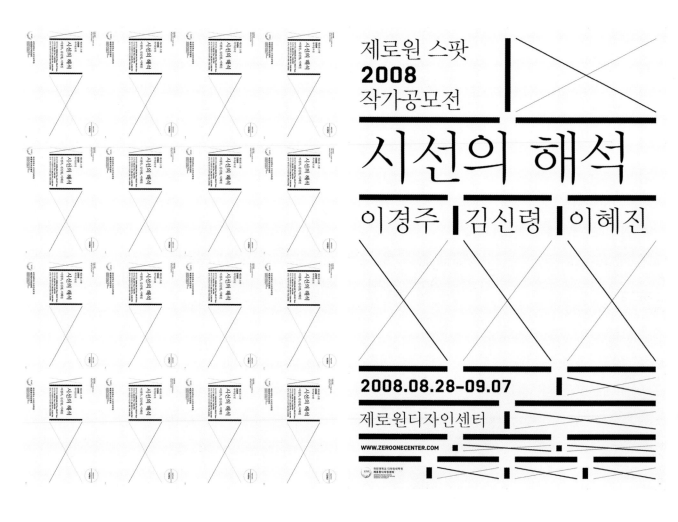

PROJECT
Zero-One Spot Exhibition,
posters, Zero-One Design
Center

COUNTRY
South Korea

YEAR
2008

DESIGN
Jae-Hyouk Sung

Project
K-SAD Workshop 27,
poster, K-SAD

Country
South Korea

Year
2009

Design
Jae-Hyouk Sung

Project
2nd Inada Stone Exhibition,
poster, Laforet

Country
Japan

Year
2006

Design
FLAME Inc.

Team
Design:
Masayoshi Kodaira
Photographer:
Naoki Ishizaka
Artist:
Silvie Freury
Producer:
Sota Futagami

PROJECT
Experience Stone Art at
Meilun, *poster*, Taiwan
Design Center

COUNTRY
Taiwan/China

YEAR
2009

DESIGN
Leslie Chan Design
Co., Ltd.

TEAM
Leslie Chan Wing Kei

PROJECT
6th Chinese Character
Festival, *poster*, Chinese
Foundation for Digitization
Technology

COUNTRY
Taiwan/China

YEAR
2009

DESIGN
Leslie Chan Design
Co., Ltd.

TEAM
Leslie Chan Wing Kei

project
Kengo Kuma + Michitaka Hirose Exhibition, *poster*, Okumura Design Space

country
Japan

year
2006

design
FLAME Inc.

team
Design:
Masayoshi Kodaira
Photographer:
Naoki Ishizaka
Artist:
Silvie Freury
Producer:
Sota Futagami

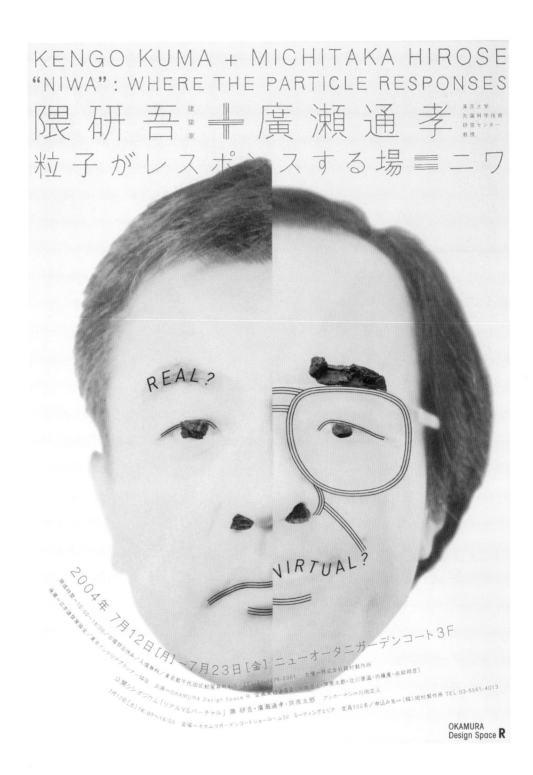

6+6 Germany and Taiwan Poster Design Exhibition
Date: May 16 to June 1, 2009 Venue: National Chiang Kai-Shek Memorial Hall (The Second Display Room), 21 Chung Shan S. Road, Taipei, Taiwan Exhibitor: GERMANY: Uwe Loesch/Chris Hinrichsen, Jianpeng He, Henning Wangerinnen, Gunter Schmidt, Gunter Karl Bose, Anggar, Ajae Lin, Peng Boseng, Yu Lang/Zeng Lin/Hong-lic, Lindie Chan, Wang-Kin, Chen Kwei Lang/Lins Lin Chuang Lang. Organizer: National Chiang Kai-Shek Memorial Hall, Taiwan Poster Design Association Sponsor: National Kaohsiung Normal University.

6+6 德國與台灣海報設計展
展覽日期:2009年5月16日起至6月1日 地點:國立中正紀念堂管理處 (瞻仰大廳)台北市中正區中山南路21號 展出者:德國:Uwe Loesch/Chris Hinrichsen、Jianpeng He、Henning、Wangerinnen、Gunter Schmidt、Gunter Karl Bose、袁廣、呂明輝、林延澤、彭柏盛、彭佳慧、林弘毅、詹麗雪等 2009年5月16日-月日09:30 參觀時間:上午09:30 下午10:00-12:00 主辦單位:國立中正紀念堂管理處、台灣海報設計協會 贊助單位:國立高雄師範大學

tpda

PROJECT
Six Plus Six, *poster*, Taiwan
Poster Design Association

COUNTRY
Taiwan/China

YEAR
2009

DESIGN
Leslie Chan Design
Co., Ltd.

TEAM
Leslie Chan Wing Kei

PROJECT
Migration Birds, *poster*,
Taiwan Poster Design
Association

COUNTRY
Taiwan/China

YEAR
2009

DESIGN
Leslie Chan Design
Co., Ltd.

TEAM
Leslie Chan Wing Kei

PROJECT
Feathers, *poster*, Taiwan
Poster Design Association

COUNTRY
Taiwan/China

YEAR
2009

DESIGN
Leslie Chan Design
Co., Ltd.

TEAM
Leslie Chan Wing Kei

PROJECT
"Industrial Pollution",
"Global Warming",
"Automotive Pollution",
posters, The China
Environment Protection
Fund

COUNTRY
China

YEAR
2009

山非山
水非水

亿万吨工业废气和废水
源源不断进入天空海洋
大自然失去永不复回
停止工业污染珍爱自然

DESIGN
JWT Shanghai

TEAM
Illustration:
Yang Yong Liang

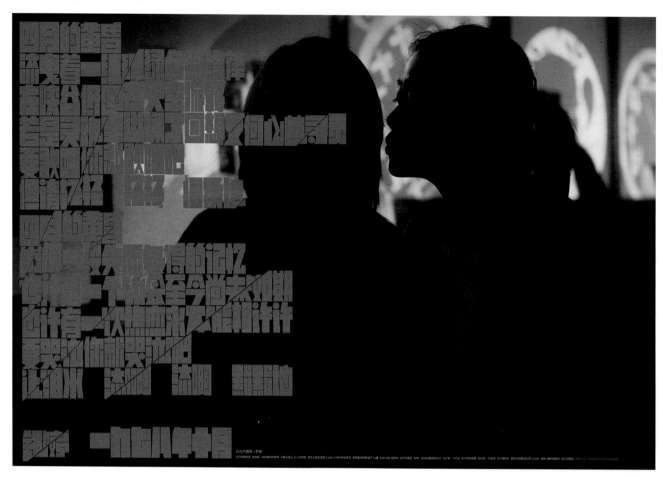

PROJECT
Chinese Type Design,
poster

COUNTRY
China

YEAR
2002

DESIGN
Ling Meng

PROJECT
Live With Art, *poster*

COUNTRY
China

YEAR
2002

DESIGN
Ling Meng

project
Chinese Type Design,
posters

country
China

year
2009

design
Ling Meng

August 6-8, 2005 Tokyo International Forum, Exhibition Hall

Open Hour: 10:00 - 20:00 (until 17:00 Last Day) Initiated by: ART FAIR TOKYO Committee Sponsored by: ITOCHU Corporation / Veolia Water Japan K.K. / M Factory Corporation
GIORGIO ARMANI JAPAN CO., LTD. / SECOM CO., Ltd. / Pictet Financial Management Consultants Co., Ltd. / MY INVESTMENTS LTD. / MONTBLANC
Supported by: The Ministry of Foreign Affairs of Japan / Ministry of Economy, Trade and Industry / The Commercial Service of the U.S. Embassy, Tokyo / Embassy of Israel / Embassy of Italy
Austrian Embassy / Royal Netherlands Embassy / Korean Cultural Service, Embassy of Korea / Embassy of the Federal Republic of Germany
Admission: 1 Day Free Pass Adult ¥1,000 / Students ¥800 / Free for children who are grade school age and younger.
Advance Ticket: 1 Day Free Pass ¥800 (Adult Only) e-plus [www.eplus.co.jp/artfair-tokyo] / Ticket Pia [P-code: 686-072 Tel: 0570-02-9999] / LAWSON TICKET [L-code: 33502 Tel: 0570-063-003]

「日本はもっとアートが好きな国になりませんか。」
「このアート、やばいよ。」「技術もすごいけれど、
考え方がすごいなあ。」「このアートを買った、という
より、やっと手に入れた。」「ココロがシーンとする
アートもあるし、ココロがザワザワするアートもある。」
「いいものを観ると、自分もがんばろうと思える。」
「ほう、あなたは、そういうアートを気に入る人でし
たか。」「どこ観てるんですか？そのアートの。」「お目
が高い、というか、お目が厳しい。」「好きなアート
や好きな人に会うと、欲しくてたまらなくなる。」
「金銭感覚がなくなる。」「この人の家には、金は
ないけど、アートならある。」「映画デートもいいけど、
アートデートもいいな、と思った。」「こういうアート
フェアが日本の文化になれるといいのだけれど。」

ART FAIR TOKYO トウキョウ

アートフェア東京　2005年 8月6日［土］・7日［日］・8日［月］　東京国際フォーラム・展示ホール

開場=10:00-20:00［最終日は17:00まで］　主催=アートフェア東京実行委員会　協賛=伊藤忠商事株式会社／ヴェオリア・ウォーター・ジャパン株式会社／株式会社エムファクトリー／ジョルジオ アルマーニ ジャパン株式会社／セコム株式会社
ピクテ ファイナンシャル マネジメント コンサルタント株式会社／MY INVESTMENTS LTD.／モンブラン（50音順）　後援=外務省／経済産業省／アメリカ合衆国大使館商務部／イスラエル大使館／イタリア大使館／オーストリア大使館
オランダ王国大使館／駐日韓国大使館 韓国文化院／ドイツ連邦共和国大使館　入場料=1DAYパスポート 一般1,000円／学生800円／小中学生以下無料（但し保護者同伴）
前売りチケット=1DAYパスポート 800円（一般のみ）　e-plus [www.eplus.co.jp/artfair-tokyo]／チケットぴあ［Pコード 686-072 Tel: 0570-02-9999］／ローソンチケット［Lコード 33502 Tel: 0570-063-003］
コンテンポラリー、モダン、アンティーク、知る人ぞ知る国内外80の有力ギャラリーが出展いたします。

お問い合わせ=アートフェア東京実行委員会事務局　〒106-0031 東京都港区西麻布1-9-11　ART FAIR TOKYO Committee 1-9-11 Nishiazabu, Minato-ku, Tokyo 106-0031 Japan Tel: 03-5771-4520 Fax: 03-3401-9038 E-mail: info@artfairtokyo.com
www.artfairtokyo.com

project
Tokyo International Forum
Art Exhibition, *poster*,
Art Fair Tokyo

country
Japan

year
2005

design
FLAME Inc.

team
Design:
Masayoshi Kodaira
Photographer:
Naoki Ishizaka
Artist:
Silvie Freury
Producer:
Sota Futagami

project
Bruce Lee, *poster*,
personal work

country
Singapore

year
2008

design
Marcus Lim

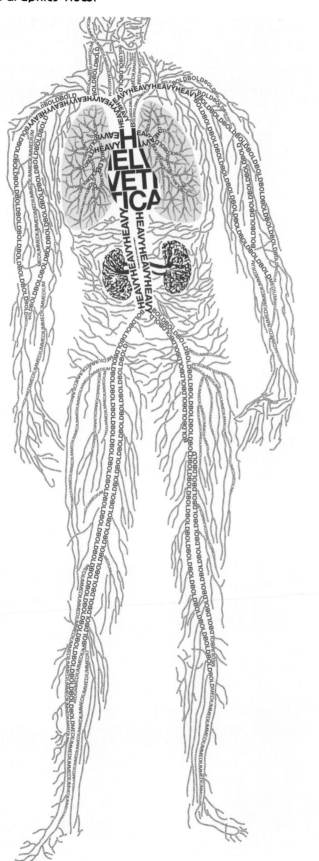

PROJECT
Helvetica, *poster*,
Helvetica Project

COUNTRY
Japan

YEAR
2008

DESIGN
FLAME Inc.

TEAM
Masayoshi Kodaira

PROJECT
Idol! Exhibition, *poster*,
Yokohama Museum of Art

COUNTRY
Japan

YEAR
2006

DESIGN
FLAME Inc.

TEAM
Masayoshi Kodaira

project
The Marvelous Night of
Seoul, *poster*, Lighting
Festival Seoul

country
South Korea

year
2007

design
Minsun Eo

project
Prototype 03, *poster*,
Prototype Exhibition
Executive Committee

country
Japan

year
2009

design
Nakano Design Office

team
Takeo Nakano

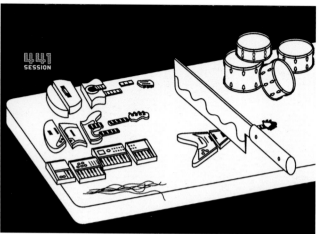

PROJECT
441 Session, *posters*

COUNTRY
Japan

YEAR
2009

DESIGN
finch-talk

TEAM
Art Direction/Design:
Nobuhiro Kobayashi
Illustration:
Naomi Nishijima

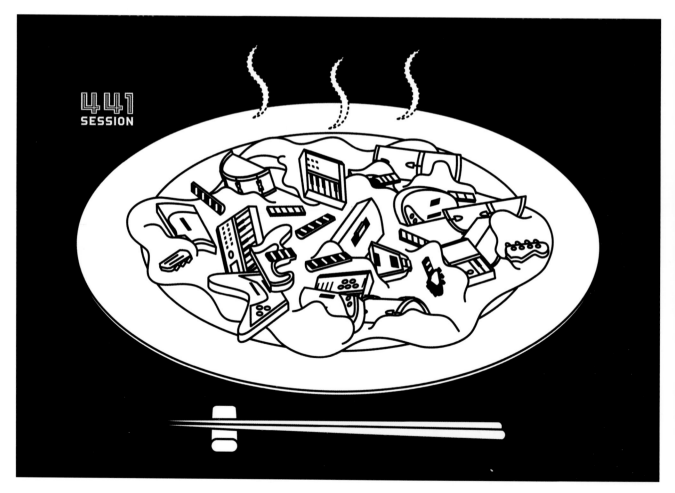

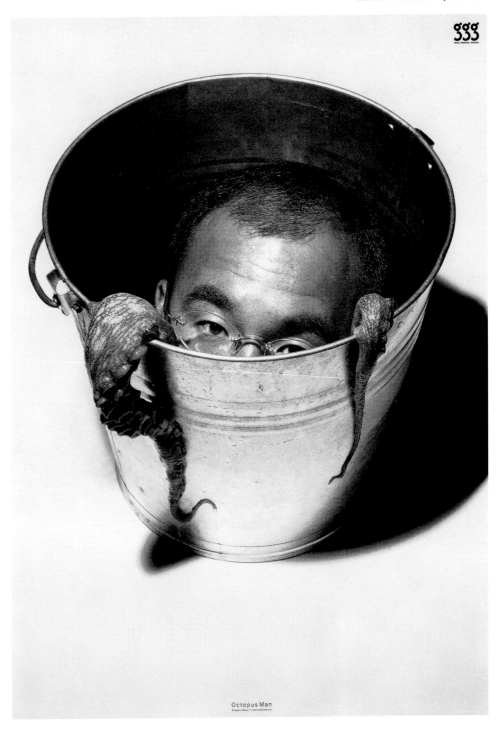

Octopus Man

PROJECT
OctopusMan, *poster*,
Ginza Graphic Gallery

DESIGN
Shinmura Design Office

COUNTRY
Japan

TEAM
Norito Shinmura

YEAR
2002

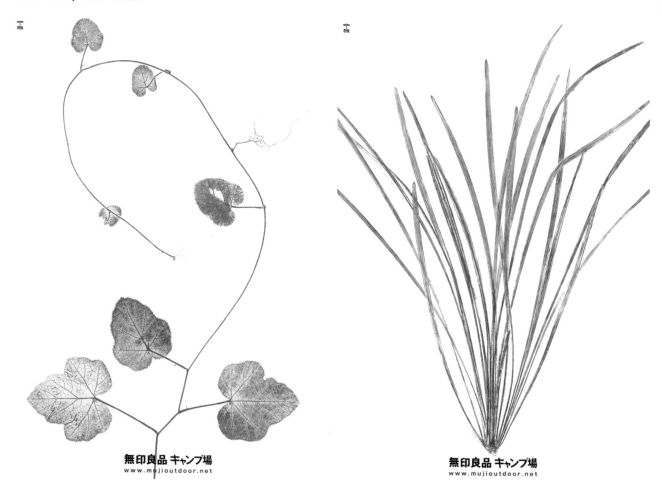

PROJECT

Muji Campsite/Leaf Print,
Insect, Tree Bark, Cloud,
posters, MUJI

COUNTRY

Japan

YEAR

2005–2007

DESIGN

Shinmura Design Office

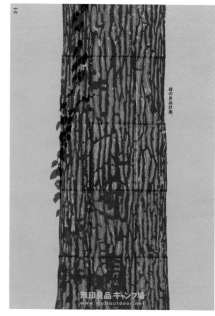

無印良品 キャンプ場
www.mujioutdoor.net

無印良品 キャンプ場
www.mujioutdoor.net

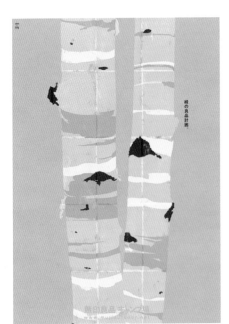

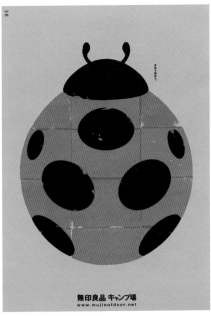

無印良品 キャンプ場
www.mujioutdoor.net

無印良品 キャンプ場
www.mujioutdoor.net

PROJECT
D&L gallery, *poster*,
Little Things Theory

COUNTRY
Taiwan/China

YEAR
2009

DESIGN
PHDC

TEAM
Po-hsuan Hsu,
Yin-wen Chen

罠で、
釣る。

漁師の島の新村水産

腕で、
釣る。

漁師の島の新村水産

頭で、
釣る。

漁師の島の新村水産

鯵は縄下や釣るんがいちばんじゃ。舟がおったら、その後ろも狙い目じゃ。

暦で、
釣る。

漁師の島の新村水産

PROJECT
Fisherman, *posters*,
Shinmura Fisheries

COUNTRY
Japan

YEAR
2004

DESIGN
Shinmura Design Office

TEAM
Norito Shinmura

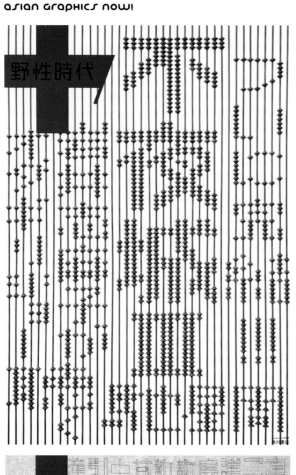

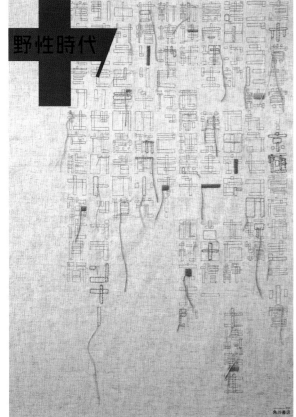

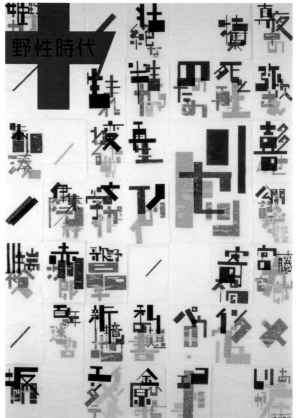

project
YASEIJIDAI, *posters*,
Kadokawa Shoten
Publishing Co., Ltd.

country
Japan

year
2004

design
Shinmura Design Office

team
Kosuke Niwano

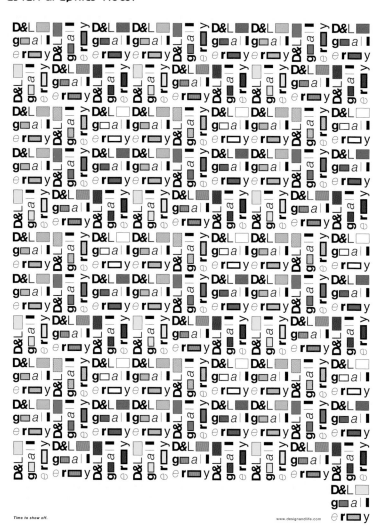

Time to show off.

www.designandlife.com

PROJECT

D&L gallery, *posters*, Design&Life Online Magazine

COUNTRY

Taiwan/China

YEAR

2009

DESIGN

PHDC

TEAM

Po-hsuan Hsu, Yin-wen Chen

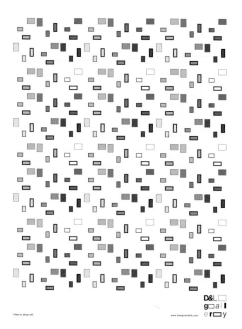

Time to show off.

www.designandlife.com

Time to show off.

www.designandlife.com

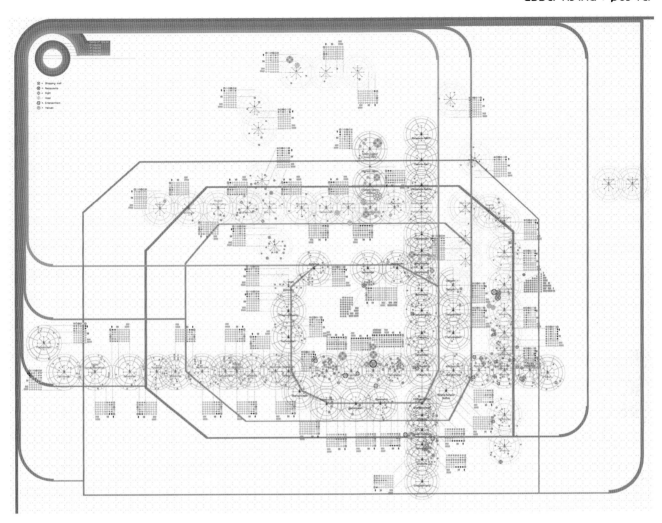

PROJECT
Beijing Map, *poster*,
What is Around

YEAR
2008

DESIGN
Penny Yu

COUNTRY
China

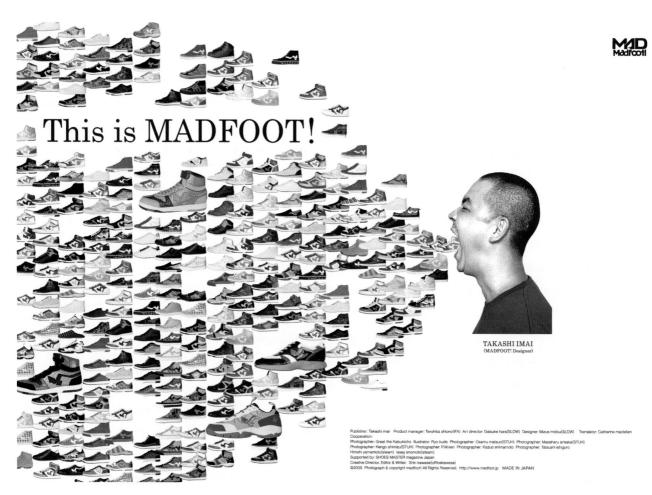

TAKASHI IMAI
(MADFOOT! Designer)

Publisher: Takashi imai   Product manager: Teruhisa shiono(IFA)   Art director: Daisuke hara(SLOW)   Designer: Mizue midoui(SLOW)   Translator: Catherine maclellan
Cooperation:
Photographer: Great the Kabukicho   Illustrator: Ryo kudo   Photographer: Osamu matsuo(STUH)   Photographer: Masaharu arisaka(STUH)
Photographer: Kengo shimizu(STUH)   Photographer: P.M.ken   Photographer: Kazuo shimamoto   Photographer: Tatsushi ishiguro
Hiroshi yamamoto(steam)   Issey enomoto(steam)
Supported by: SHOES MASTER magazine Japan
Creative Director, Editor & Writer: Shin kawase(officekawase)
©2009 Photograph & copyright madfoot! All Rights Reserved. http://www.madfoot.jp   MADE IN JAPAN

PROJECT
Madfoot! Catalog, *poster*,
Madfoot!

COUNTRY
Japan

YEAR
2009

DESIGN
SLOW Inc.

TEAM
Miwa Tokiko

PROJECT
Laforet: 30 Years Into
the Future, *catalog*,
Laforet Harajuku Co., Ltd.

COUNTRY
Japan

YEAR
2008

DESIGN
FLAME Inc.

TEAM
Art Direction/Design/Copy:
Masayoshi Kodaira
Photographer:
Mikiya Takimoto
Illustrator:
Shigeki Yuriko Yamane
Producer:
Sota Futagami

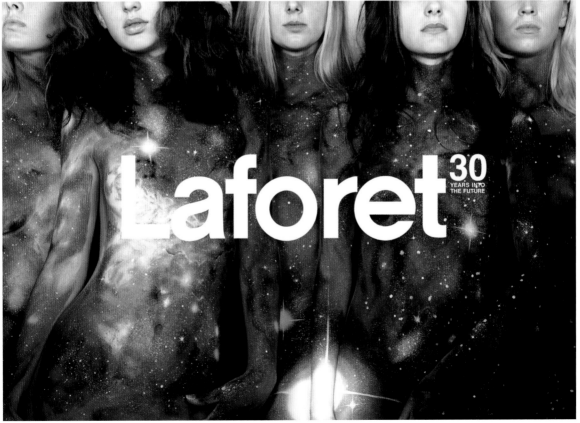

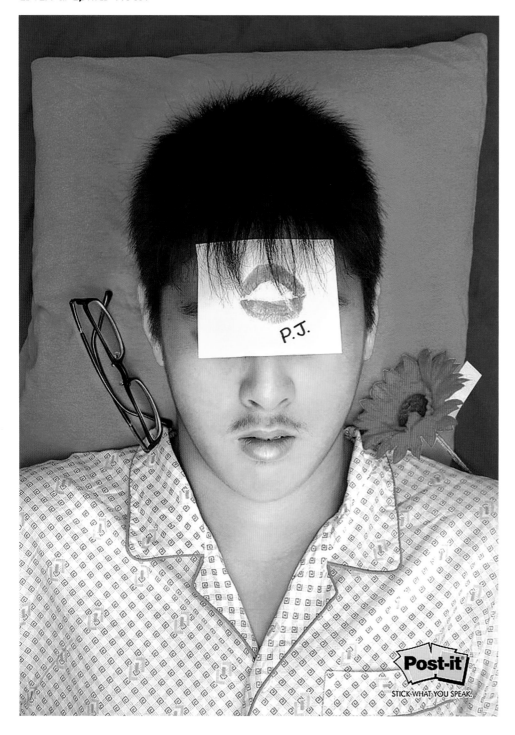

project
Spice & Herb series,
advertising,
S&B Foods Inc.

country
Japan

year
2006

design
Taku Satoh Design
Office Inc.

team
Taku Satoh

project
Stick What You Speak,
advertising, Post-it

country
Singapore

year
2007

design
PixelPastry

team
Lim Si Ping

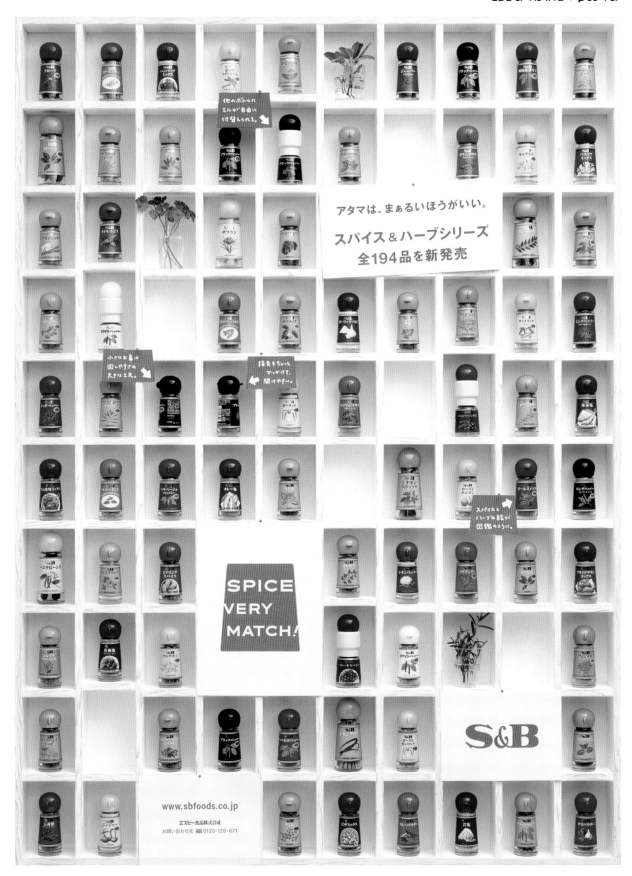

project

Issey Miyake Pleats Please,
posters, Issey Miyake Inc.

country

Japan

year

2005

design

Taku Satoh Design
Office Inc.

team

Taku Satoh

PLEATS PLEASE ISSEY MIYAKE   http://store.pleatsplease.com   AVAILABLE ON LINE, DELIVERY IN JAPAN ONLY
TOKYO ≈ Place Minami-Aoyama 3-13-21 Minami-Aoyama, Minato-ku, Tokyo Phone : 03.5772.7750 • PARIS ≈ 201
Boulevard Saint Germain, 75007 Paris Phone : 01.45.48.10.44 ≈ 3Bis Rue des Rosiers, 75004 Paris Phone : 01.40.29.99.66
• NEW YORK ≈ 128 Wooster Street, New York, NY 10012 Phone : 212.226.3600 ≈ tribeca ISSEY MIYAKE 119 Hudson Street,
New York, NY 10013 Phone : 212.226.0100 • LONDON ≈ 20 Brook Street, London W1K 5DE Phone : 020.7495.2306

PLEATS PLEASE ISSEY MIYAKE   http://store.pleatsplease.com   AVAILABLE ON LINE, DELIVERY IN JAPAN ONLY
TOKYO ≈ Place Minami-Aoyama 3-13-21 Minami-Aoyama, Minato-ku, Tokyo Phone : 03.5772.7750 • PARIS ≈ 201
Boulevard Saint Germain, 75007 Paris Phone : 01.45.48.10.44 ≈ 3Bis Rue des Rosiers, 75004 Paris Phone : 01.40.29.99.66
• NEW YORK ≈ 128 Wooster Street, New York, NY 10012 Phone : 212.226.3600 ≈ tribeca ISSEY MIYAKE 119 Hudson Street,
New York, NY 10013 Phone : 212.226.0100 • LONDON ≈ 20 Brook Street, London W1K 5DE Phone : 020.7495.2306

PLEATS PLEASE ISSEY MIYAKE   http://store.pleatsplease.com   AVAILABLE ON LINE, DELIVERY IN JAPAN ONLY
TOKYO ≈ Place Minami-Aoyama 3-13-21 Minami-Aoyama, Minato-ku, Tokyo Phone : 03.5772.7750 • PARIS ≈ 201
Boulevard Saint Germain, 75007 Paris Phone : 01.45.48.10.44 ≈ 3Bis Rue des Rosiers, 75004 Paris Phone : 01.40.29.99.66
• NEW YORK ≈ 128 Wooster Street, New York, NY 10012 Phone : 212.226.3600 ≈ tribeca ISSEY MIYAKE 119 Hudson Street,
New York, NY 10013 Phone : 212.226.0100 • LONDON ≈ 20 Brook Street, London W1K 5DE Phone : 020.7495.2306

PLEATS PLEASE ISSEY MIYAKE   http://store.pleatsplease.com   AVAILABLE ON LINE, DELIVERY IN JAPAN ONLY
TOKYO ≈ Place Minami-Aoyama 3-13-21 Minami-Aoyama, Minato-ku, Tokyo Phone : 03.5772.7750 • PARIS ≈ 201
Boulevard Saint Germain, 75007 Paris Phone : 01.45.48.10.44 ≈ 3Bis Rue des Rosiers, 75004 Paris Phone : 01.40.29.99.66
• NEW YORK ≈ 128 Wooster Street, New York, NY 10012 Phone : 212.226.3600 ≈ tribeca ISSEY MIYAKE 119 Hudson Street,
New York, NY 10013 Phone : 212.226.0100 • LONDON ≈ 20 Brook Street, London W1K 5DE Phone : 020.7495.2306

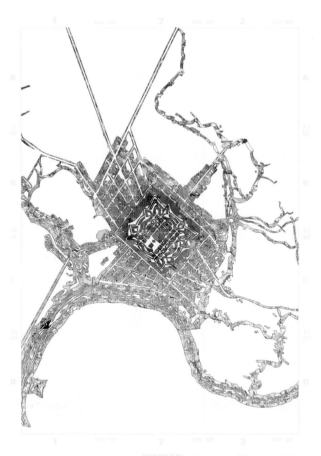

PROJECT
GridCell385, *posters*,
Personal work

COUNTRY
Vietnam

YEAR
2008

DESIGN
Tan Dat Nguyen

PROJECT
Internet Nature
Information System,
"Mizugashima", *online
campaign*, Ministry of the
Environment Government
of Japan

COUNTRY
Japan

YEAR
2004

DESIGN
Chihiro Katoh

TEAM
Art Direction:
Yumi Sakai (NHK Art, Inc.);
Design:
Mai Uchikune
(System Shiki)
Illustrator:
Chihiro Katoh
Editor:
Shigeo Takagi
(System Shiki)
Creative Director:
Shunji Satoh
(NHK Art, Inc.)
Planning:
Japan Water
Clean Association

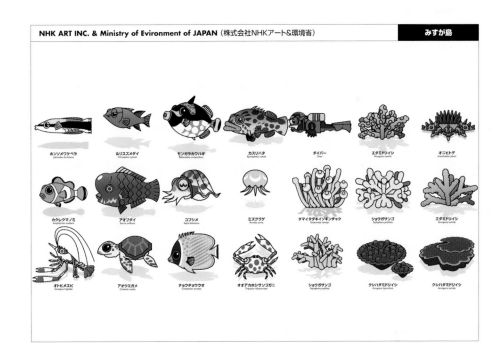

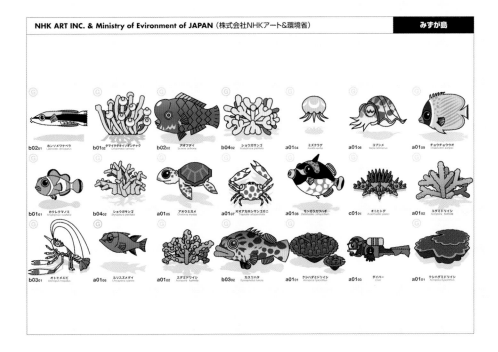

project
Converse Fall '09 Lyrics
Campaign, advertising
campaign, Converse

country
China

year
2009

design
Wieden + Kennedy
Shanghai

team
Creative Director:
Nick Barham
Creative Leader:
Julie Liu
Art Director:
Tea Qiu
Design:
Momo Wu, Greg Sun,
Leal Bao, Morris Lee
Copy:
Matthew Carey, Lulu Xu
Account:
Anne Halvorson, Kei Chan,
Vivian Chen, Jamie Han
Producer:
Angie Wong, Julia Liu

NIKEBASKETBALL.COM.CN

PROJECT
LeBron James MVP
Quickstrike, *advertising*,
Nike China

COUNTRY
China

YEAR
2009

DESIGN
Wieden + Kennedy
Shanghai

TEAM
Executive Creative Director:
Nick Cohen
Art Director:
Justin Hays
Copy:
Zebra Hua
Account Manager:
Chris Dixon
Design:
Nelson Ng, Kevin Cao
Illustration:
Elephant Xiang
*Nike Brand
Connections Director:*
Kerri Hoyt-Pack
*Nike Brand
Connections Manager:*
Sukwan Chae

PROJECT
Nike Air Max LeBron VII,
advertising, Nike China

COUNTRY
China

YEAR
2009

DESIGN
Wieden + Kennedy
Shanghai

TEAM
Executive Creative Director:
Nick Cohen
Art Director:
Gino Woo,
Emilia Bergmans
Copy:
Thomas Tsang, Cook Xu
Design:
Keith Wang

Illustration:
Ling Meng, Sally Zou,
Radio Woo
Account Manager:
Chris Dixon
Nike Brand
Connections Manager:
Sukwan Chae

PROJECT
Nike Sportswear FA09
AW77, *online campaign*,
Nike China

COUNTRY
China

YEAR
2009

DESIGN
Wieden + Kennedy
Shanghai

TEAM
Creative Director:
Conan Wang, Gino Woo
Design:
Elephant Xiang, Ling Meng
Copy:
Allen Feng, Cook Xu,
Lulu Xu
Account Service:
Jason White, Gavin Lum,
Susie Ni
Planner:
Nick Barham, Dominic Tan
Printer Corp:
Jackie Liang, Keith Wang
Photography:
Timothy Saccenti
Programming:
Francis Lam, Yang Mo,
Jeff Yan
Producer:
Kerli, Celes, Ivy, Rain,
Xiuhong, Mud

project

"b+ab/Spring & Summer",
"b+ab/Fall&Winter",
posters, I.T.apparels
limited, b + a b

country

Japan

year

2009 and 2007

design

Yuni Yoshida

team

Art Direction:
Yuni Yoshida
Hair & Make-up:
Shinji Konishi
Spring & Summer
Photographer:
Muga Miyahara
Stylist:
Yuya
Fall&Winter
Photographer:
Shoji Uchida
Stylist:
Yuka Ogura

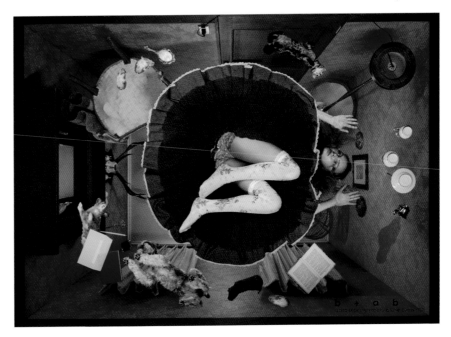

project

Bless China – Sichuan
Earthquake 512, *poster*,
New Graphic Magazine
China

country

Hong Kong/China

year

2008

design

Ameba Design

team

Gideon Lai, Thor

project

Loving Embrace., *poster*,
Department of Commercial
Affairs, MOEA. China Prod

country

Taiwan/China

year

2009

design

Human Paradise Studio

team

Brad Tzou

project

Love is Hope, *poster*, RCM
Art Museum Nanjing

country

China

year

2008

design

Chen Zhengda

Loving Embrace

PROJECT
+ (plus), *posters*,
Glasshouse Sugahara

COUNTRY
Japan

YEAR
2009

DESIGN
iyamadesign inc.

TEAM
Koji Iyama

PROJECT
We're one, *poster*, Taiwan
International Poster Design
Award 2007

COUNTRY
Hong Kong/China

YEAR
2007

DESIGN
Ameba Design

TEAM
Gideon Lai, Vincent

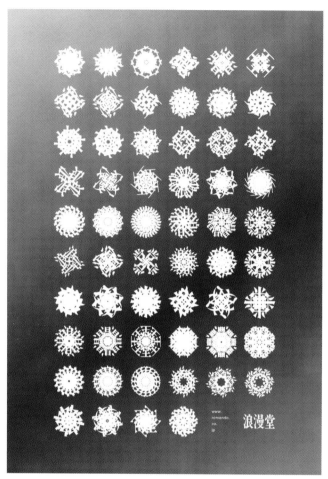

PROJECT
Romando Representative
Director, *posters*

COUNTRY
Japan

YEAR
2007

DESIGN
Romando Co., Ltd.

TEAM
Art Direction/Design:
Kyosuke Tsuji
Creative Director:
Takashi Kamada

FUKUOKA **VISIONARY**ARTS
Food Create Department
pâtissier, bakery, café

学校法人 福岡安達学園
専門学校 福岡ビジョナリーアーツ
フードクリエイト学科

PROJECT
Visionary Arts Guide Book,
posters, Royal Arts

COUNTRY
Japan

YEAR
2009

DESIGN
SLOW Inc.

TEAM
Daisuke Hara

FUKUOKA **VISIONARY**ARTS
Pet Department
dog grooming, dog trainer, animal health technician,
companion animal welfare, pet business, pet food, cat master

学校法人 福岡安達学園
専門学校 福岡ビジョナリーアーツ
ペット学科

FUKUOKA **VISIONARY**ARTS
Wedding Produce Department
wedding planner, bridal beauty, house wedding

学校法人 福岡安達学園
専門学校 福岡ビジョナリーアーツ
ウェディングプロデュース学科

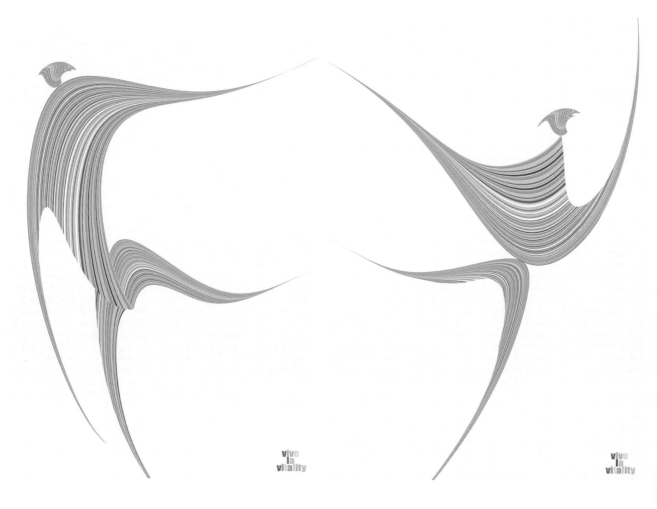

PROJECT
Vive la vitality., *posters*,
Department of Commercial
Affairs, MOEA. China Prod

COUNTRY
Taiwan/China

YEAR
2006

DESIGN
Human Paradise Studio

TEAM
Brad Tzou

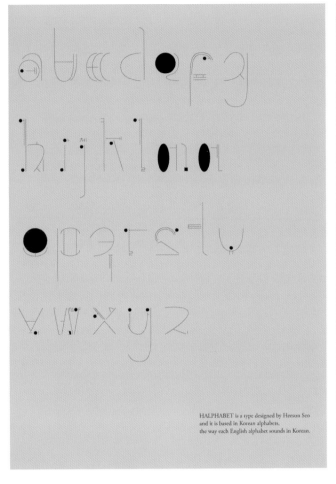

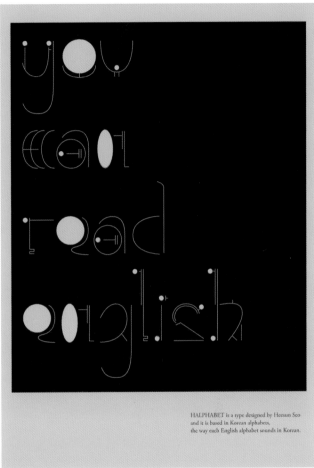

PROJECT
Halphabet, *posters*,
personal work

COUNTRY
South Korea

YEAR
2009

DESIGN
Heesun Seo

PROJECT
WWF, *outdoor advertising*

YEAR
2006

COUNTRY
China

DESIGN
Pan Jianfeng

PROJECT
PSP, *outdoor advertising,*
Sony Computer
Entertainment

COUNTRY
Japan

YEAR
2005

DESIGN
MR_DESIGN

TEAM
Art Direction:
Kenjiro Sano
Design:
Koichi Kosugi

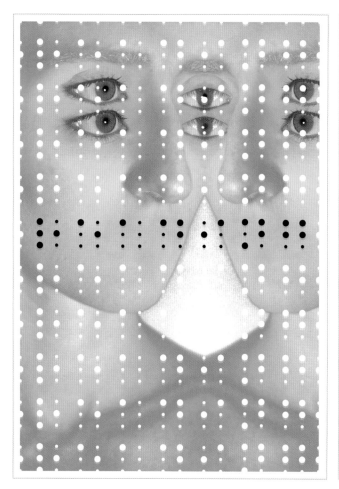

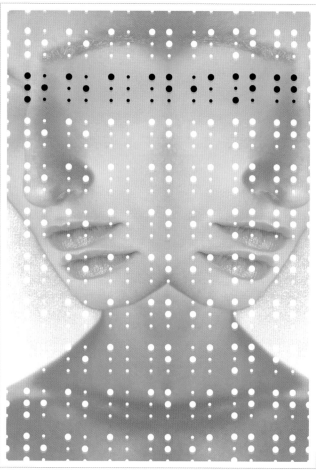

PROJECT
Reading, *posters*, Taiwan
Poster Design Association

COUNTRY
Taiwan/China

YEAR
2008

DESIGN
Human Paradise Studio

TEAM
Design/Photography:
Brad Tzu
Model:
Cara Speckhals

PROJECT
Form Texture, *posters*

COUNTRY
Japan

YEAR
2009

DESIGN
iyamadesign inc.

TEAM
Koji Iyama

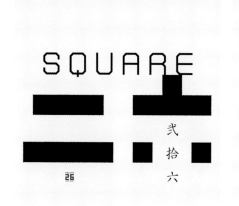

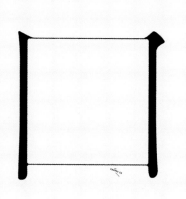

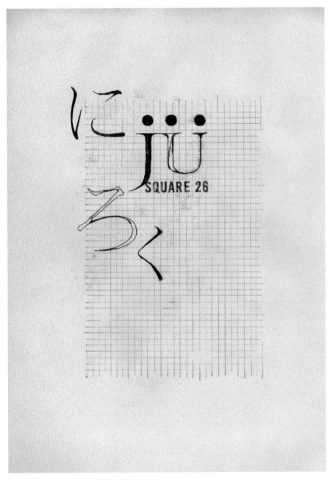

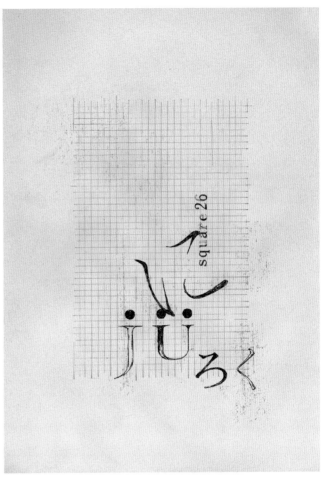

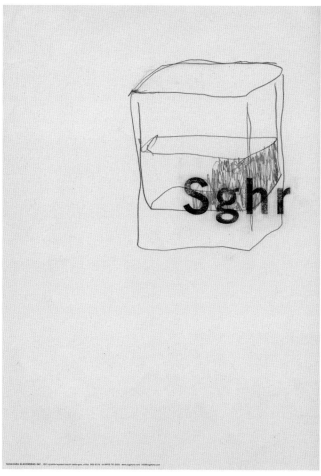

PROJECT
Handmade, *posters,*
Sugahara Glassworks Inc.

COUNTRY
Japan

YEAR
2006

DESIGN
iyamadesign inc.

TEAM
Art Direction/Design:
Koji Iyama
Illustration:
Yoshiko Akado

SUGAHARA GLASSWORKS INC.
797 fujishita kujukuri-machi
sanbu-gun, chiba. 283-0112
tel:0475-76-3551 www.sugahara.com
info@sugahara.com

SUGAHARA GLASSWORKS INC.
797 fujishita kujukuri-machi
sanbu-gun, chiba. 283-0112
tel:0475-76-3551 www.sugahara.com
info@sugahara.com

SUGAHARA GLASSWORKS INC.
797 fujishita kujukuri-machi
sanbu-gun, chiba. 283-0112
tel:0475-76-3551 www.sugahara.com
info@sugahara.com

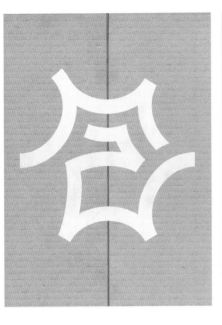

PROJECT
Pack, *posters*, Keiwa
Packages

COUNTRY
Japan

YEAR
2005

DESIGN
iyamadesign inc.

TEAM
Koji Iyama

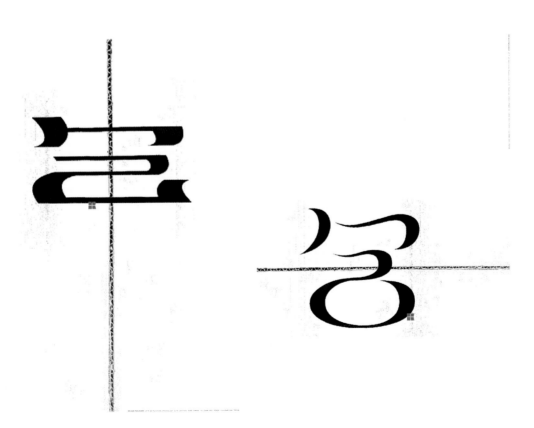

project
Graduation Show, *poster*,
personal work

country
South Korea

year
2009

design
Heesun Seo

team
Heesun Seo, Eunsang Lee,
Hwanuk Choe, Qjin Cho

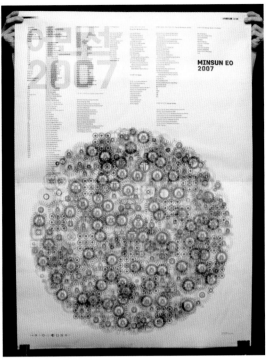

PROJECT
Minsun Eo 2007, *poster*,
personal work

COUNTRY
South Korea

YEAR
2007

DESIGN
Minsun Eo

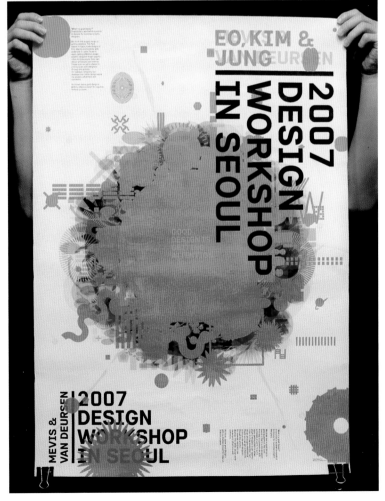

PROJECT
Smap and Hotpepper,
advertising campaign,
Recruit

COUNTRY
Japan

YEAR
2006

DESIGN
Creative Power Unit

TEAM
Ryosuke Murai

PROJECT

National Brand Change
Campaign, *magazine
advertising*, Panasonic
Corporation

COUNTRY

Japan

YEAR

2008

DESIGN

Creative Power Unit

TEAM

Hisato Takagi

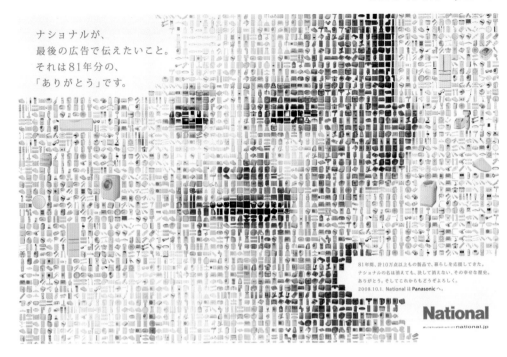

PROJECT

Kotori, *online campaign*,
Fostex

COUNTRY

Japan

YEAR

2009

DESIGN

IMG SRC

TEAM

Hiroshi Koike, Tatsuaki
Ashikaga, Izumi Horio,
Tatsuhiko Akutsu,
Atsushi Fujimaki,
Aya Iwasaki (SUN-AD),
Hiroaki Kitamura,
Sakuya Nishiyama,
Yasutaka Kurihara,
Yasutaka Yamasaki, Asial,
S2Factory, FLAME, BILCOM

project
"Comic storyteller in kagurazaka (2010)", "Picasso De Festa (2009)", "Face (2003)", "U.G. Sato's Visual structure (2003)", *posters*

country
Japan

year
2003–2010

design
U.G. Sato

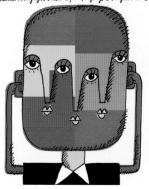

The tree is full of life.

PROJECT
Japanese Sake, *poster*

COUNTRY
Japan

YEAR
1985

DESIGN
U.G. Sato

PROJECT
Treedom, *poster*

COUNTRY
Japan

YEAR
1993

DESIGN
U.G. Sato

PROJECT
Manners, *posters*, Metro Cultural Foundation

COUNTRY
Japan

YEAR
2008

DESIGN
Bunpei Ginza

TEAM
Bunpei Yorifuji

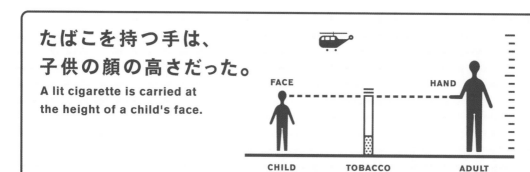

家でやろう。
Please do it at home.

 車内でのお化粧はご遠慮ください。
Please refrain from putting on make-up in the train.

家でやろう。
Please do it at home.

 座席の独り占めはご遠慮ください。
Please share the seat with others.

PROJECT
Smoking Manners, *posters*,
Japan Tobacco Inc.

COUNTRY
Japan

YEAR
2010

DESIGN
Bunpei Ginza

TEAM
Bunpei Yorifuji,
Takuya Shibata

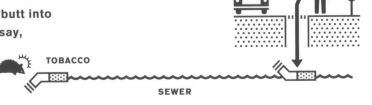

吸いがらを排水溝に捨てた。
というか隠した。

I threw my cigarette butt into
the drain. That is to say,
I hid it in the drain.

あなたが
気づけば
マナーは
変わる。

MORE INFO → www.jti.co.jp

The Art

branding

PROJECT
Eye Place,
corporate identity

COUNTRY
Singapore

YEAR
2006

DESIGN
&Larry

TEAM
Creative Director:
Larry Peh
Design:
Ter Yeow Yeong

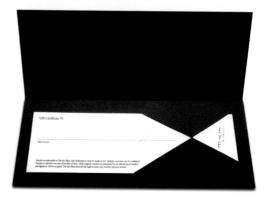

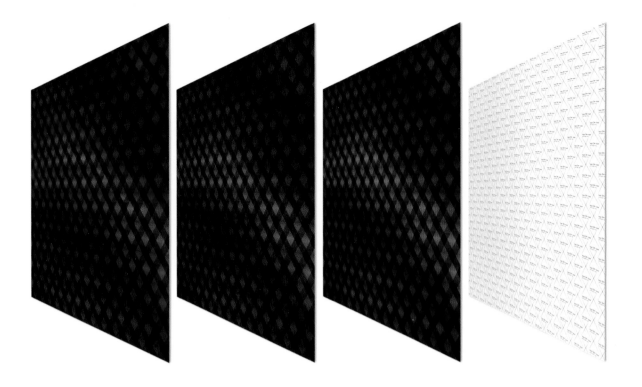

PROJECT
iFourum, *branding
campaign*, Toshin
Development Co., Ltd.

COUNTRY
Singapore

YEAR
2006–2009

DESIGN
&Larry

TEAM
Creative Director:
Larry Peh
Design:
Larry Peh, Ter Yeow Yeong,
Adora Tan
Illustration:
Larry Peh, Ter Yeow Yeong,
Flee Circus
Photography:
DC Chang

PROJECT
iFourum, *branding campaign*, Toshin Development Co., Ltd.

COUNTRY
Singapore

YEAR
2006–2009

DESIGN
&Larry

TEAM
Creative Director:
Larry Peh
Design:
Larry Peh, Ter Yeow Yeong, Adora Tan
Illustration:
Larry Peh, Ter Yeow Yeong, Flee Circus
Photography:
DC Chang

CHRISTMAS RE-IMAGINED
FOURUM
• LEVEL 4 • TOWER B • TAKASHIMAYA S.C.

This Christmas, surprise and delight your loved ones with a selection of thoughtful and expressive gifts, many lovingly crafted by hand from around the world. Come up to iFourum at Takashimaya Shopping Centre L4 and discover gifts of art that everyone can enjoy.

THE GIFT OF ART

- ART FRIEND
- BOOKBINDERS DESIGN
- CREATIVE HANDS
- L'ESCALIER
- MERLIN FRAME MAKER & ART GALLERY
- STUDIO MIU
- THE BETTER GIFT STORE
- THE BETTER TOY STORE

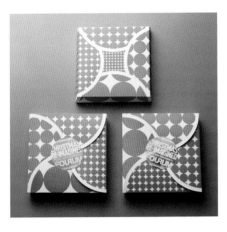

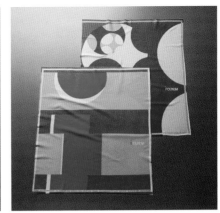

PROJECT
iFourum, *branding campaign*, Toshin Development Co., Ltd.

COUNTRY
Singapore

YEAR
2006–2009

DESIGN
&Larry

TEAM
Creative Director:
Larry Peh
Design:
Larry Peh, Ter Yeow Yeong, Adora Tan
Illustration:
Larry Peh, Ter Yeow Yeong, Flee Circus
Photography:
DC Chang

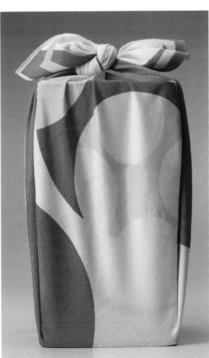

PROJECT
The Marmalade Pantry,
corporate identity

COUNTRY
Singapore

YEAR
2009

DESIGN
&Larry

TEAM
Creative Director:
Larry Peh
Design:
Lee Weicong

PROJECT
Wooonderland,
corporate identity

COUNTRY
Singapore

YEAR
2006

DESIGN
&Larry

TEAM
Creative Director:
Larry Peh
Design:
Ter Yeow Yeong

project
20/20 Base, *exhibition,*
publication and branding,
Design Singapore Council

country
Singapore

year
2007

design
Black Design

team
Jackson Tan, Tanny Wong,
Natalie Seng

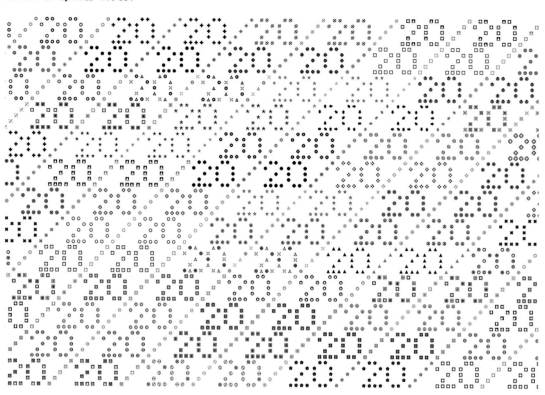

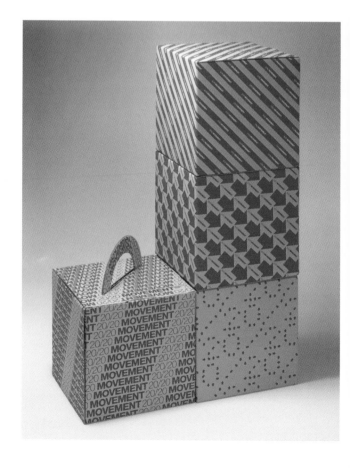

PROJECT
20/20 Movement,
*exhibition, publication
and branding*, Design
Singapore Council

COUNTRY
Singapore

YEAR
2006

DESIGN
Black Design

TEAM
Jackson Tan, Sijia Lim

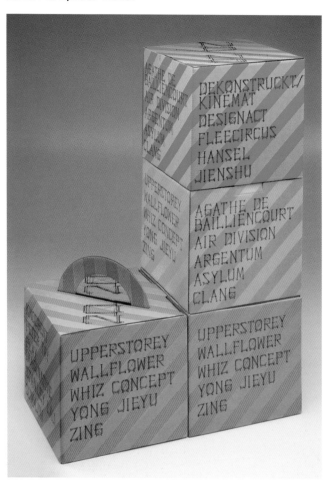

PROJECT
20/20 Under Construction, *exhibition, publication and branding*, Design Singapore Council

COUNTRY
Singapore

YEAR
2005

DESIGN
Black Design

TEAM
Jackson Tan, Sijia Lim

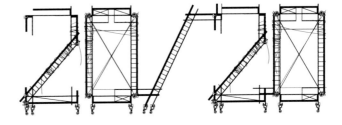

PROJECT
Design Difference, *corporate identity*, Design Singapore Council

COUNTRY
Singapore

YEAR
2009

DESIGN
Black Design

TEAM
Jackson Tan

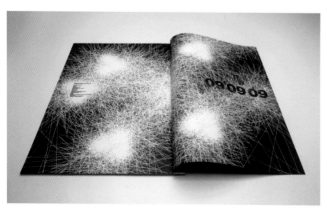

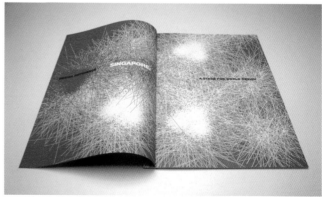

This is
Utterubbish
a collection of uselessideas

PROJECT
UseLess Exhibitions,
brand identity, Utterubbish

COUNTRY
Singapore

YEAR
2008

DESIGN
Black Design

TEAM
Jackson Tan,
Tanny Wong

UseLess Life

UseLess Life

無用生活
UseLess Life

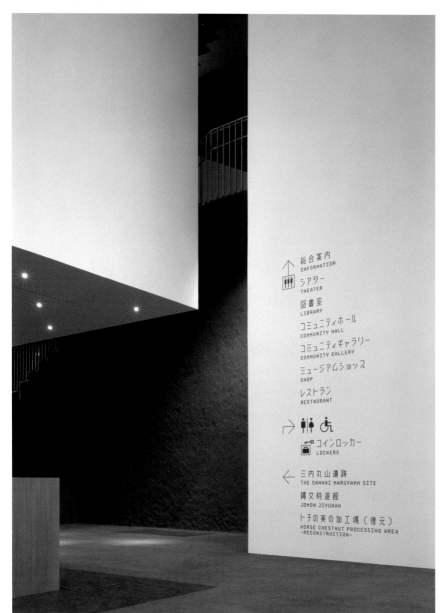

PROJECT
Aomori Museum of
Art, *corporate identity
and signage*, Aomori
Prefectural Government

COUNTRY
Japan

YEAR
2006

DESIGN
Bluemark Inc.

TEAM
Art Direction:
Atsuki Kikuchi
Design:
Atsuki Kikuchi,
Shoichiro Moriya,
Tilmann S. Wendelstein,
Shinji Nemoto

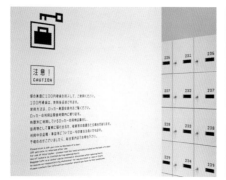

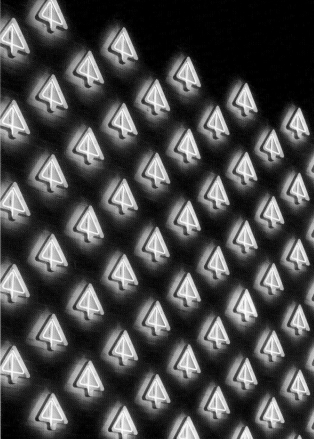

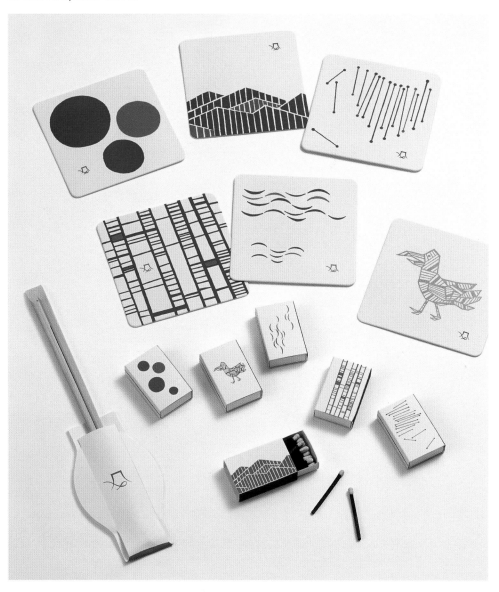

PROJECT
HUMOR, *corporate identity and packaging*, Huit Inc.

COUNTRY
Japan

YEAR
2007

DESIGN
Bluemark Inc.

TEAM
Art Direction/Design:
Atsuki Kikuchi
Designer:
Atsuki Kikuchi,
Tilmann S. Wendelstein

PROJECT
Go-Fu-Jyu-U, *corporate identity and tableware*

COUNTRY
Japan

YEAR
2005

DESIGN
Bluemark Inc.

TEAM
Art Direction/Design:
Atsuki Kikuchi
Printing Director:
Takashi Ochiai

PROJECT
Enigma Fitness,
brand identity

COUNTRY
India

YEAR
2009

DESIGN
Codesign

TEAM
Rajesh Dahiya,
Hanumant Khanna

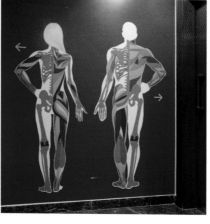

Run

Harder » Further » Longer

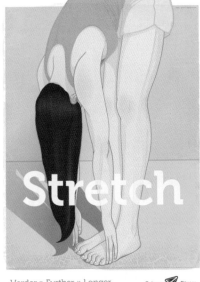

Stretch

Harder » Further » Longer

Push

Harder » Further » Longer

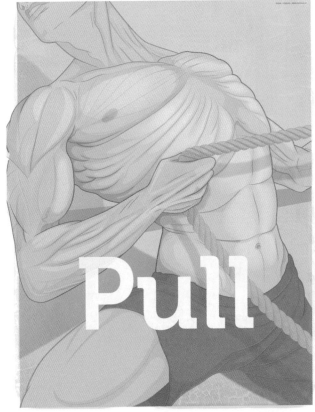

Pull

Harder » Further » Longer

Breathe

Deeper » Purer » Longer

PROJECT
House This!,
brand identity

COUNTRY
India

YEAR
2008

DESIGN
Codesign

TEAM
Rajesh Dahiya,
Hanumant Khanna

 + + + =

Heart	**Water**	**Fire**	**Leaf**
Love	Peace	Warmth	Growth
Affection	Freedom	Cosy	Life
Care	Tranquility	Protection	Sustenance

PROJECT
Pouss Pouss,
brand identity,
Feiyue Shoes

COUNTRY
China

YEAR
2008

DESIGN
Harigata

TEAM
Adrien Nazez,
Jean Christophe Naour

8:Shenton
Singapore 068808

Breakfast

Lunch

Drinks

Dinner

PROJECT
8 Shenton, *brand identity and interior design*, CBRE Richard Ellis

COUNTRY
Singapore

YEAR
2009

DESIGN
Designphase

TEAM
Branding:
Fearghal Hendron
Interior Design:
Joris Angevaare
3D:
Mel Quinola

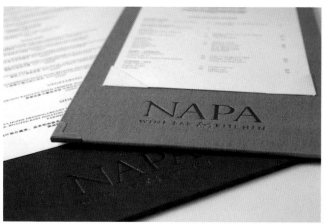

PROJECT
Napa Wine Bar & Kitchen,
*corporate identity and
packaging, Menu*

COUNTRY
China

YEAR
2009

DESIGN
Thread Design Shanghai

TEAM
Evelyn Hussain

NAPA
WINE BAR & KITCHEN

PROJECT
Simply Sandwich,
brand identity

COUNTRY
Singapore

YEAR
2008

DESIGN
Epigram

TEAM
Creative Director:
Edmund Wee
Design Director:
Zann Wan

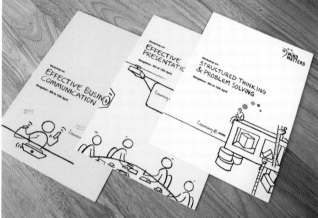

PROJECT
Mind Matters,
corporate identity

COUNTRY
India

YEAR
2009

DESIGN
Exit Design

TEAM
Karn Malhotra,
Tharakaram,
Tabish Shakil

DAOiSM

DONALD DAViS

ART AND THE ART OF LIFE

Lecture 2 / 26 / 2009

Thursday, 7:00–8:30 p.m.
The Baron and Ellin Gordon Art Galleries
Old Dominion University
4509 Monarch Way at 45th Street

Workshop 03 / 02 / 2009

Monday, 6:00–9:00 p.m.
Visual Arts Building, Room #216
Old Dominion University
Art Department, 49th Street

Details

Attendance at the lecture is a prerequisite
for participation in the workshop.
Preregistration is required. Please email or call.
awhelan@odu.edu (757) 685.1981.

PROJECT
Daoism: Donald Davis,
visual identity, Old
Dominion University

COUNTRY
South Korea

YEAR
2009

DESIGN
Jiwon Lee

PROJECT
Lee Kuan Yew World City
Prize, *corporate identity*,
The Urban Redevelopment
Authority

YEAR
2009

DESIGN
H55

COUNTRY
Singapore

TEAM
Creative Director:
Hanson Ho

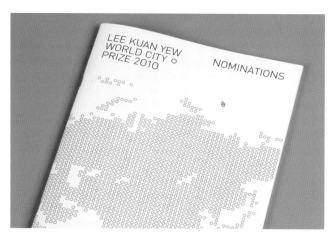

LEE KUAN YEW
WORLD CITY ○
PRIZE 2010

LEE KUAN YEW
WORLD CITY ○
PRIZE 2016

LEE KUAN YEW
WORLD CITY ○
PRIZE 2012

LEE KUAN YEW
WORLD CITY ○
PRIZE 2018

LEE KUAN YEW
WORLD CITY ○
PRIZE 2014

LEE KUAN YEW
WORLD CITY ○
PRIZE 2020

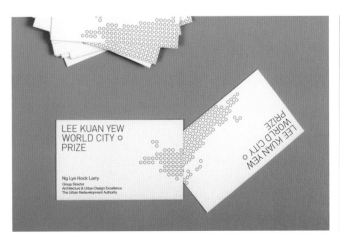

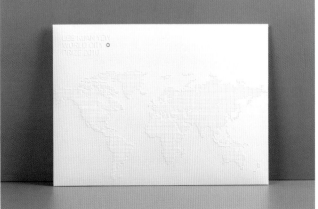

PROJECT
The Sandwich Shop,
corporate identity

COUNTRY
Singapore

YEAR
2003

DESIGN
H55

TEAM
Creative Director:
Hanson Ho

PROJECT

NewWave Exhibition,
corporate identity

COUNTRY

Singapore

YEAR

2008

DESIGN

Black Design

TEAM

Jackson Tan, Tanny Wong

Project
19th Macao Arts Festival,
corporate identity, Cultural
Affairs Bureau of Macao
S.A.R. Government

Country
Macao/China

Year
2008

Design
Hong Chong Ip

Team
Hong Chong Ip,
Victor Hugo Marreiros,
Leong Chi Hang
Illustration:
Hong Chong Ip
Photography:
Hong Chong Ip

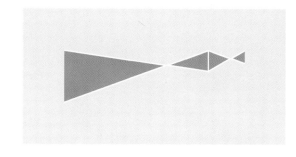

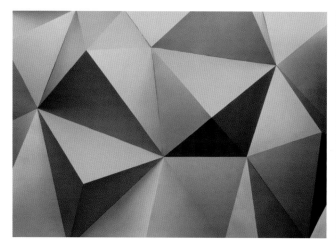

PROJECT
19th Macao Arts Festival, *corporate identity*, Cultural Affairs Bureau of Macao S.A.R. Government

COUNTRY
Macao/China

YEAR
2008

DESIGN
Hong Chong Ip

TEAM
Hong Chong Ip,
Victor Hugo Marreiros,
Leong Chi Hang
Illustration:
Hong Chong Ip
Photography:
Hong Chong Ip

PROJECT
20th Macao Arts Festival,
corporate identity, Cultural
Affairs Bureau of Macao
S.A.R. Government

COUNTRY
Macao/China

YEAR
2009

DESIGN
Hong Chong Ip

TEAM
Hong Chong Ip,
Victor Hugo Marreiros,
Leong Chi Hang
Illustration:
Hong Chong Ip,
Ha Tin Cheong;
Photography:
Hong Chong Ip

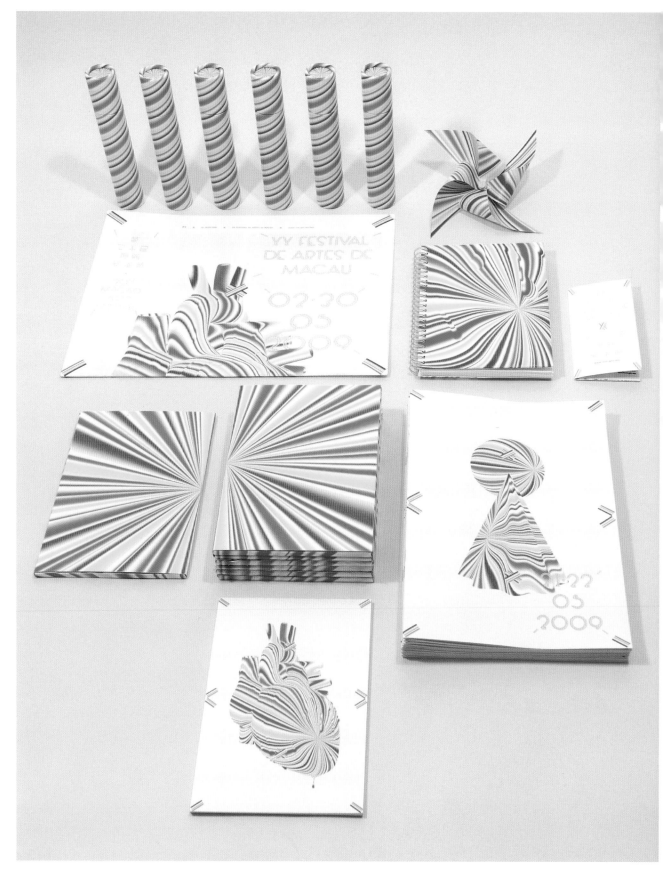

PROJECT

20th Macao Arts Festival, *corporate identity*, Cultural Affairs Bureau of Macao S.A.R. Government

COUNTRY

Macao/China

YEAR

2009

DESIGN

Hong Chong Ip

TEAM

Hong Chong Ip,
Victor Hugo Marreiros,
Leong Chi Hang
Illustration:
Hong Chong Ip,
Ha Tin Cheong
Photography:
Hong Chong Ip

PROJECT
22nd Macao International
Music Festival, *corporate
identity*, Cultural Affairs
Bureau of Macao S.A.R.
Government

COUNTRY
Macao/China

YEAR
2008

DESIGN
Hong Chong Ip

TEAM
Hong Chong Ip,
Victor Hugo Marreiros,
Leong Chi Hang
Illustration:
Hong Chong Ip
Photography:
Hong Chong Ip

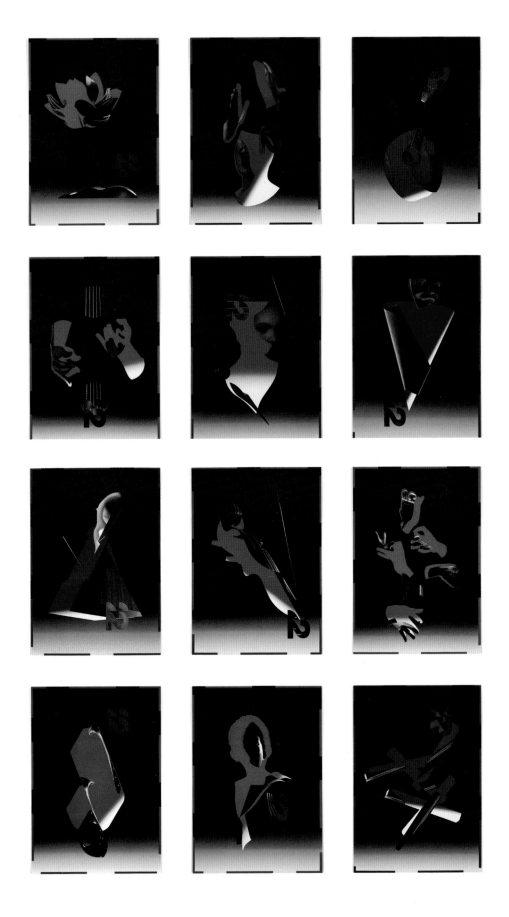

PROJECT

Mela, *brand identity*

COUNTRY

India

YEAR

2009

DESIGN

Ishan Khosla Design

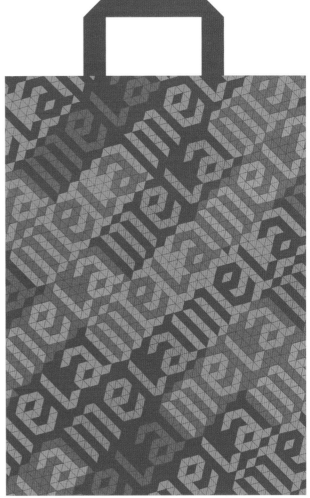

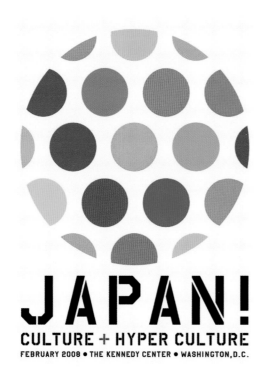

PROJECT
Japan Festival, *visual identity*, The Kennedy Center Washington, D.C.

COUNTRY
Japan

YEAR
2007

DESIGN
Hakuhodo Inc.

TEAM
Art Direction:
Kenjiro Sano
Design:
Ryota Sakae,
Kotaro Hattori

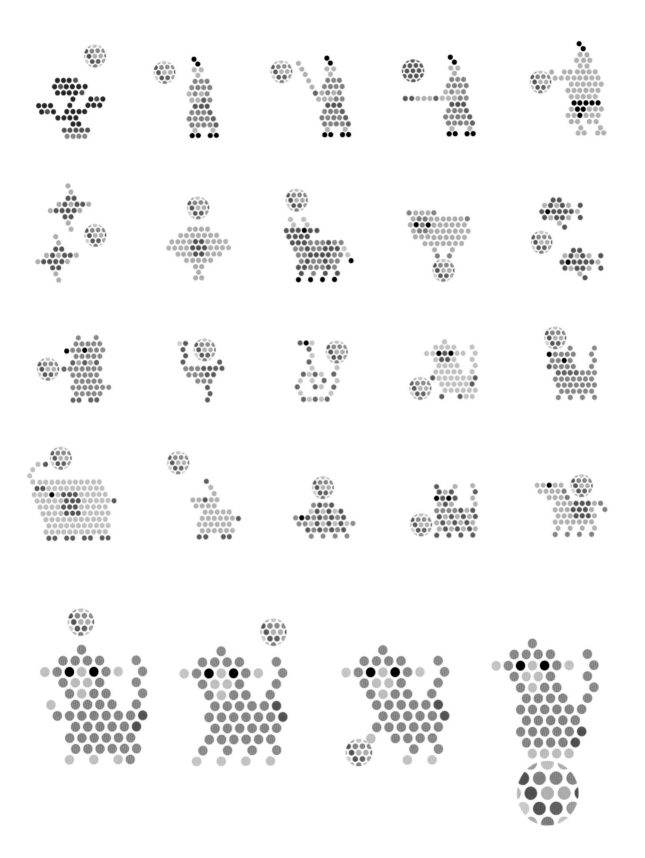

project

mt masking tape,
brand identity,
Kamoi Kakoshi

country

Japan

year

2009

design

iyamadesign inc.

team

Koji Iyama, Yoshiko Akado,
Mayuko Watanabe,
Mayu Yamaura

rhythm™
PRESIDENT'S LECTURE 2009

project
Rhythm, Lasalle President's Lecture 2009, *visual identity*, Lasalle College of the Arts

year
2009

design
Marcus Lim

country
Singapore

PRESIDENT'S LECTURE 2009

ADMISSION TICKET

DATE **10 Sept 09**

DAY **Thursday**

TIME **4 pm**

VENUE **The Singapore Airlines Theatre (Basement 1), LASALLE College of the Arts**

Please be seated by **3.45pm**

DATE/TIME **Thurs 10 Sept 09 at 4pm**

VENUE **Singapore Airlines Theatre (Basement 1) of LASALLE College of the Arts**

As seats are limited, **please register at** The **LASALLE** Library or the **Division of Student Services** for your tickets.

Buffet reception will be held for all members of the audience after the lecture.

PROJECT
MTV Asia Awards 2009,
visual identity, Student
Project

COUNTRY
Singapore

YEAR
2009

DESIGN
Marcus Lim

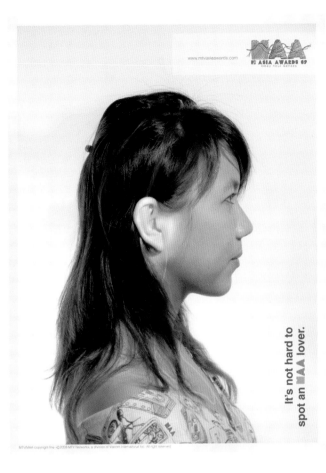

It's not hard to spot an MAA lover.

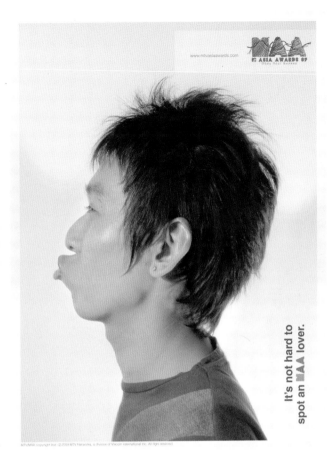

It's not hard to spot an MAA lover.

STLYE GUIDE

project
MTV Asia Awards 2010,
visual identity, Student
Project

country
Singapore

year
2009

design
Marcus Lim

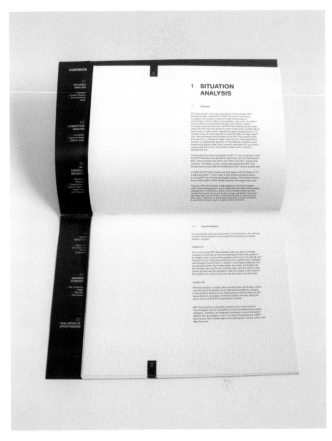

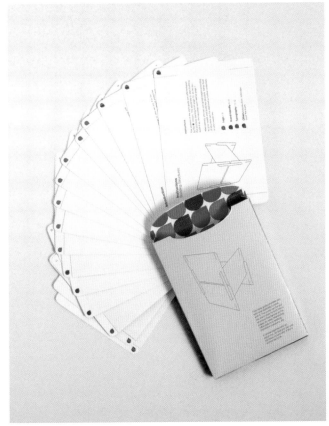

Dream
Museum
Convenience
Store

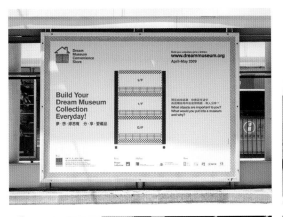

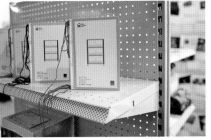

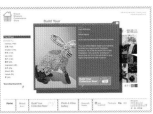

PROJECT
Dream Museum
Convenience Store,
brand identity,

COUNTRY
Hong Kong/China

YEAR
2009

DESIGN
Milkxhake

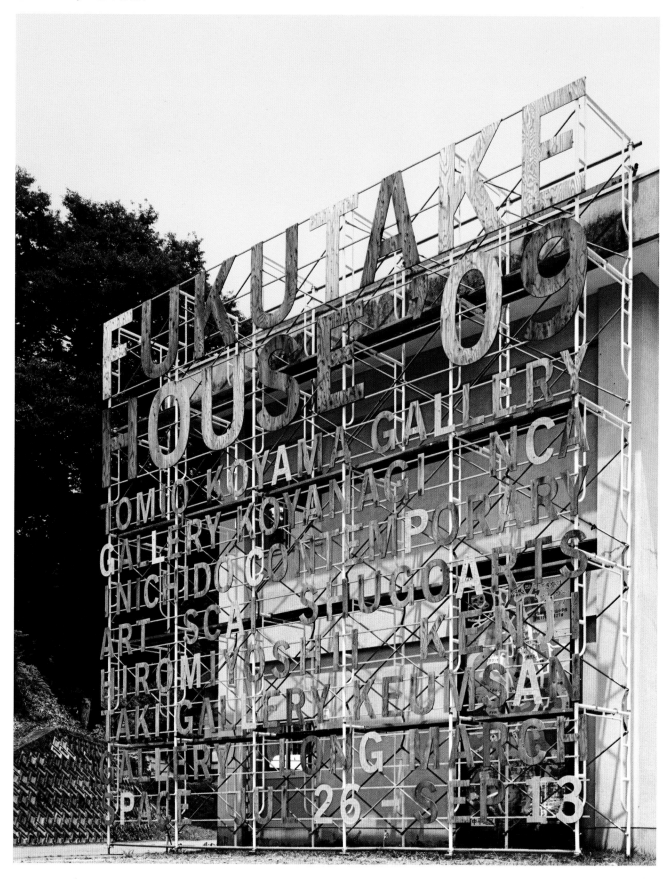

PROJECT
Fukutake House 2009,
*visual identity and
exhibition signage*,
Fukutake Foundation
for the Promotion
of Regional Culture

COUNTRY
Japan

YEAR
2009

DESIGN
FLAME Inc.,
E.P.A.

TEAM
Art Direction/Design:
Masayoshi Kodaira
Design:
Yukiharu Takematsu
Producer:
Soichiro Fukutake

Photography:
Mikiya Takimoto,
Fumihito Katamura

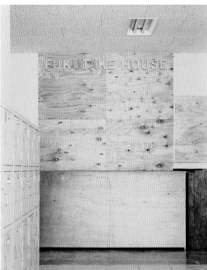
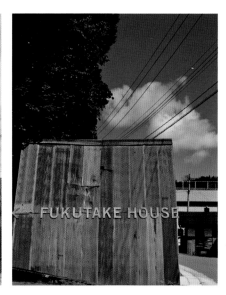

PROJECT
Shifting Sites: Cultural Desire and the Museum, *visual Identity*, Asia Art Archive

DESIGN
Milkxhake

TEAM
Javin Mo

COUNTRY
Hong Kong/China

YEAR
2008

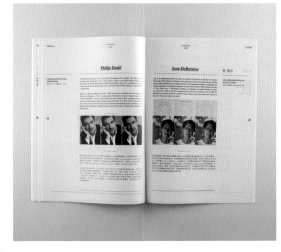

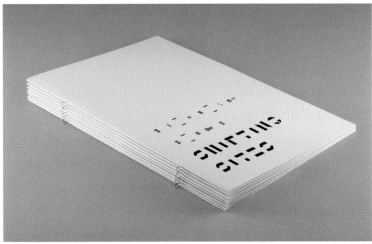

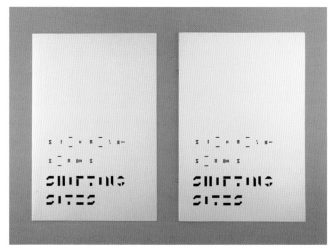

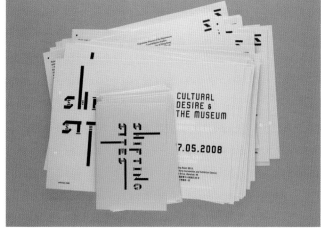

PROJECT
Mirowave International
New Media Arts
Festival 2008 "Transient
Creatures", *visual identity*

COUNTRY
Hong Kong/China

YEAR
2009

DESIGN
Milkxhake

TEAM
Javin Mo

PROJECT
21_21 Design Sight,
branding design,
21_21 Design Sight Inc.

COUNTRY
Japan

YEAR
2007

DESIGN
Taku Satoh Design
Office Inc.

TEAM
Taku Satoh

project
21_21 Design Sight
Exhibition "Water",
*exhibition and
branding design*

country
Japan

year
2007

design
Taku Satoh Design
Office Inc.

team
Taku Satoh

water

PROJECT

Cleansui, *brand identity*,
Mitsubishi Rayon
Cleansui Co., Ltd.

COUNTRY

Japan

YEAR

2009

DESIGN

Taku Satoh Design
Office Inc.

TEAM

Taku Satoh

PROJECT
Chocolate Research Facility,
brand identity and interior design

COUNTRY
Singapore

YEAR
2008

DESIGN
Asylum Creative

TEAM
Creative Direction:
Chris Lee
Design:
Ng Chee Yong
Interior Design:
Cherin Tan

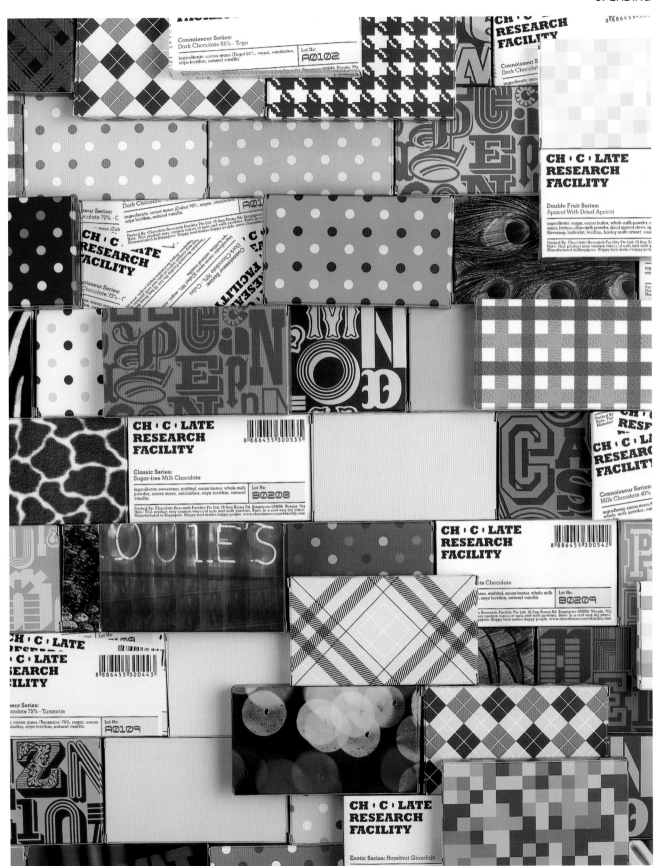

PROJECT
Chocolate Research Facility, *brand identity and interior design*

COUNTRY
Singapore

YEAR
2008

DESIGN
Asylum Creative

TEAM
Creative Direction:
Chris Lee
Design:
Ng Chee Yong
Interior Design:
Cherin Tan

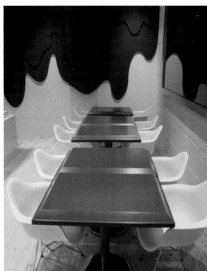

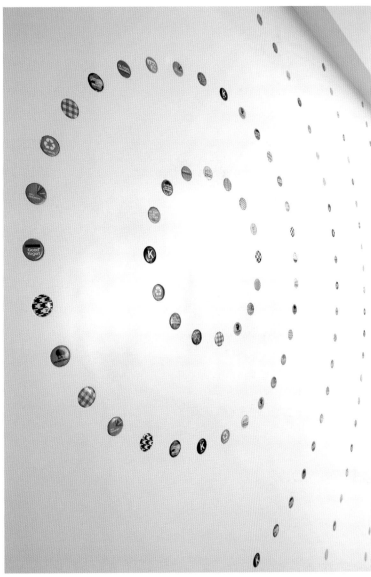

PROJECT

Frolick, *brand identity and interior design*

COUNTRY

Singapore

YEAR

2008

DESIGN

Asylum Creative

TEAM

Creative Direction:
Chris Lee
Design:
Edwin Tan

project
Ruhaak, *corporate identity*,
Christina Ruhaak Design

country
Thailand

year
2009

design
TNOP Design

team
Tnop Wangsillapakun

Nike+ アバター run run ran!

PROJECT
Nike+ Avatar Run Run Ran!, *character design*, Nike Japan Corp.

COUNTRY
Japan

YEAR
2008–2009

DESIGN
Tarout

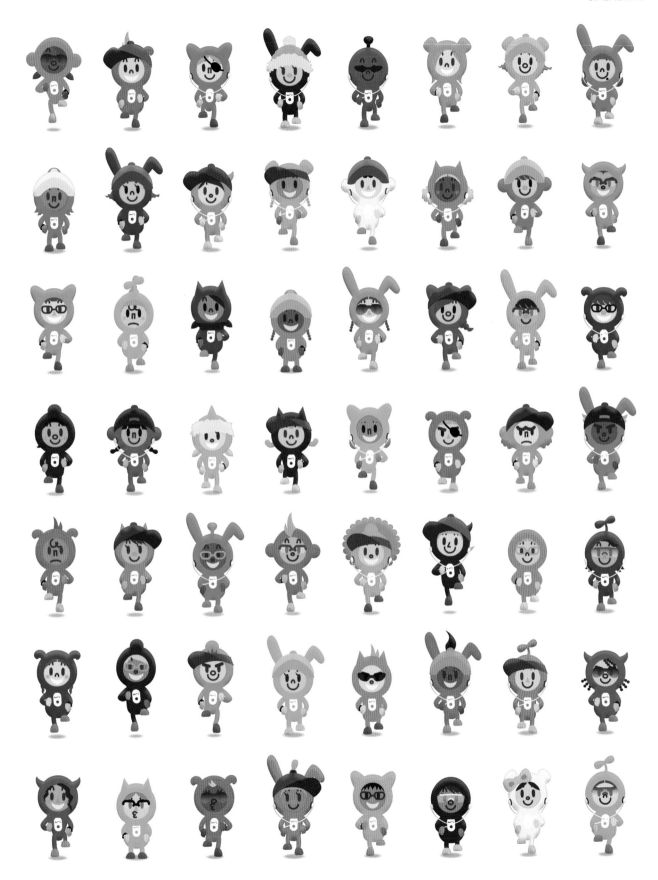

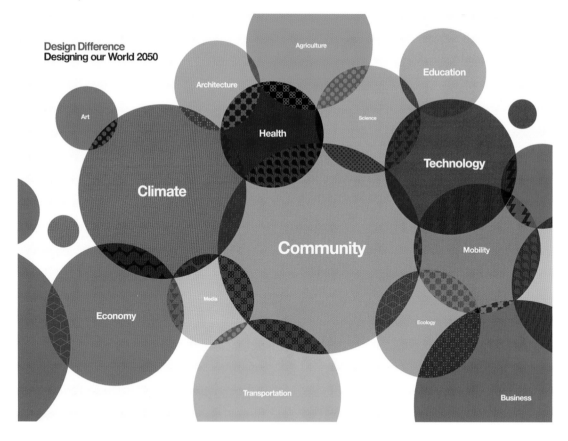

Design Difference
Designing our World 2050

Art · Architecture · Agriculture · Education · Science · Health · Climate · Technology · Community · Mobility · Economy · Media · Ecology · Transportation · Business

PROJECT
Icsid World Design
Congree 2009, *visual
identity*, Design Singapore
Council

COUNTRY
Singapore

YEAR
2009

DESIGN
Black Design

TEAM
Jackson Tan, Sumi Hie

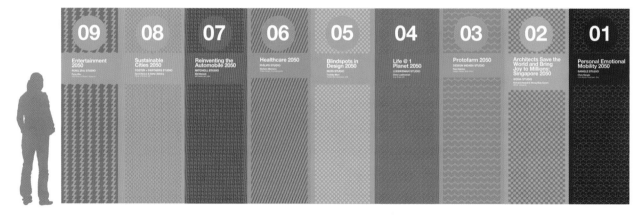

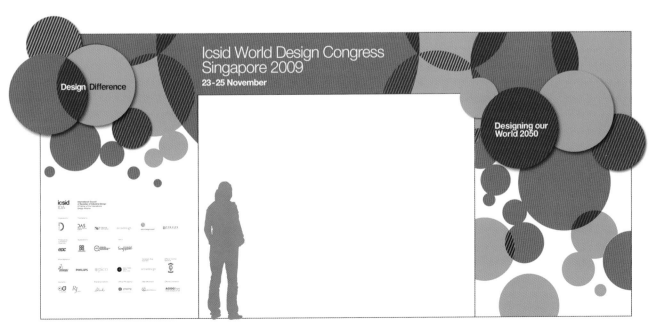

PROJECT
Evangel College,
corporate identity

COUNTRY
Hong Kong/China

YEAR
2005

DESIGN
Ameba Design

TEAM
Gideon Lai, Kenji

PROJECT
Danamon, *corporate identity*, Bank Danamon Indonesia

COUNTRY
Indonesia

YEAR
2006

DESIGN
BD+A Design

project
100% Pure, 100%
Milk, *brand identity and
packaging*, personal work

country
China

year
2009

design
Yuzhou Liu

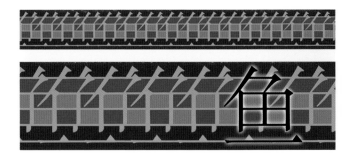

project
Design_the_Underground,
visual identity, Student
Project

country
Singapore

year
2008

design
Marcus Lim

project
Hotarumachi, *brand
identity and signage*,
Hotarumachi Building

country
Japan

year
2008

design
FLAME Inc.

team
Art Direction/Design:
Masayoshi Kodaira

THE

EDITORIAL

PROJECT
2note: time-space,
book design

COUNTRY
South Korea

YEAR
2001

DESIGN
601bisang

TEAM
Art Direction/Design/
Photography:
Kum-jun Park
Design:
Seung-youn Nam,
Jung-won Lee

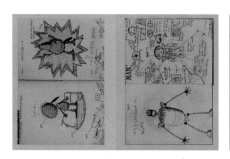

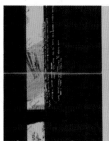

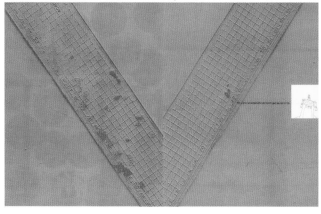
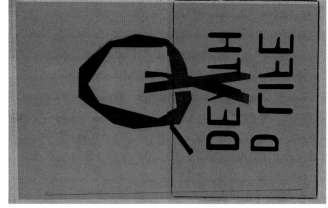

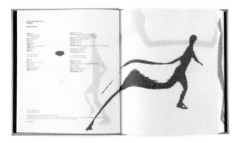

PROJECT
VIDAK 10th Anniversary
Korea Visual
Communication Design
Festival 2004, *book design*,
VIDAK (Visual Information
Design Association of
Korea)

COUNTRY
South Korea

YEAR
2004

DESIGN
601bisang

TEAM
*Art Direction/Design/
Illustration:*
Kum-jun Park

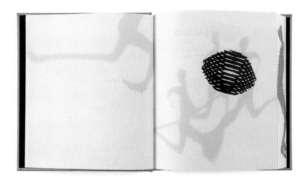

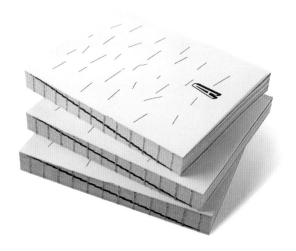

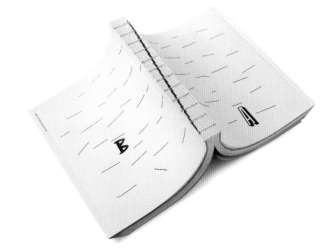

PROJECT
601 Artbook Project 2008,
book design

COUNTRY
South Korea

YEAR
2008

DESIGN
601bisang

TEAM
*Art Direction/Design/
Illustration:*
Kum-jun Park

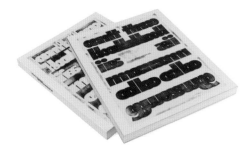

PROJECT
601 Artbook Project 2007,
book design

COUNTRY
South Korea

YEAR
2007

DESIGN
601bisang

TEAM
*Art Direction/Design/
Illustration:*
Kum-jun Park

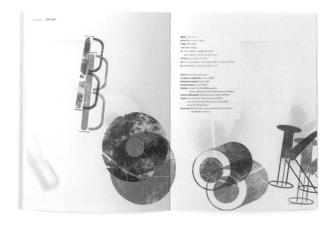

PROJECT
601 Artbook Project 2009,
book design

COUNTRY
South Korea

YEAR
2009

DESIGN
601bisang

TEAM
*Art Direction/Design/
Illustration:*
Kum-jun Park

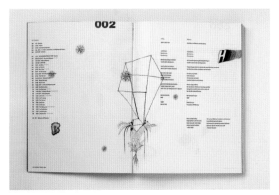

PROJECT
EOUREUM
"The Uniting of Two",
book design

COUNTRY
South Korea

YEAR
2006

DESIGN
601bisang

TEAM
*Art Direction/Design/
Illustration:*
Kum-jun Park
Calligrapher:
Yong-jin Seuk

PROJECT
Taiwan International Poster
Design Award, *book
design*, Taiwan Poster
Design Association

COUNTRY
Taiwan/China

YEAR
2005

DESIGN
Leslie Chan Design
Co., Ltd.

TEAM
Leslie Chan Wing Kei

PROJECT
GLAM magazine covers,
magazine design, BluInc
Media

COUNTRY
Singapore

YEAR
2006–2010

DESIGN
Clanhouse

TEAM
Design:
Cheah Wei Chun
Photography:
Bustamam Mokhtar
Editor:
Wirda Adnan

GAYA LEBIH ANGGUN MEWAH

GLAM

JAN 2008

SUPERGLAM 2008
FESYEN TERHANGAT & TERKINI

SIAPA DIA 20 WANITA TERKAYA DUNIA?

KORNER MAK DATIN: DATUK DENGAN SKANDAL SEKS BERAMAI-RAMAI

NASHA AZIZ SENSASI, SEKSI & DEDIKASI

GAYA LEBIH ANGGUN MEWAH

GLAM

JUL 2008

OH SO GLAM!
NORYN AZIZ
BERCAKAP TENTANG CINTA & HARI ESOK

20 LELAKI PALING SEKSI DUNIA

SPECIAL:
NEW LOOKS
FESYEN SEGAR DARI PARIS, MILAN, LONDON & NEW YORK

KORNER MAK DATIN: DERITA & SEKSA JIWA PEREMPUAN SIMPANAN DATUK

GAYA LEBIH ANGGUN MEWAH

GLAM

SYAFINAZ! REVOLUSI FESYEN! KORNER MAK DATIN! KHAS FASHION LOVES ART!

GAYA LEBIH ANGGUN MEWAH

GLAM

FESYEN POP!
GAYA & WARNA TERHANGAT DARI PARIS & MILAN

SARIMAH IBRAHIM

GAYA LEBIH ANGGUN MEWAH

loves Chanel

GLAM

GAYA LEBIH ANGGUN MEWAH

GLAM

MALAYSIA'S MOST GLAM 2008!
VANIDA IMRAN

247

PROJECT
IdN magazine,
magazine design

COUNTRY
Hong Kong/China

YEAR
1992–2010

DESIGN
IdN

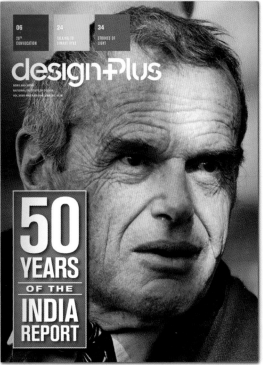

PROJECT
Design Plus, *magazine design*, National Institute of Design

COUNTRY
India

YEAR
2007

DESIGN
dev kabir malik * design

TEAM
Dev Kabir Malik

PROJECT
Dekko magazine,
Inspirational Design in
India, *magazine design*,
Codesign

COUNTRY
India

YEAR
2008

DESIGN
Codesign

TEAM
Rajesh Dahiya, Sujay
Sanan, Abhishek Ghate,
Mohor Ray

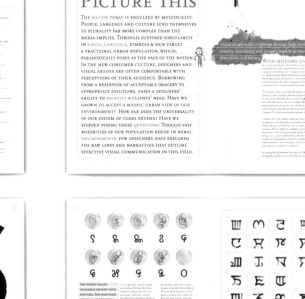

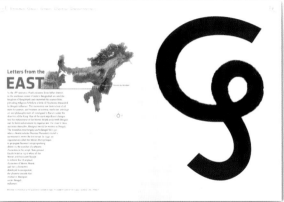

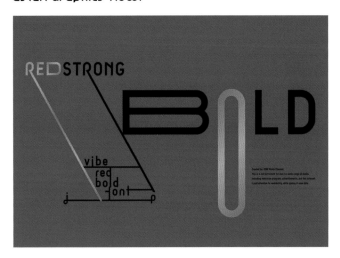

ABCDEFGHIJK
LMNOPQRSTU
VWXYZ
abcdefghijklmn
opqrstuvwxyz
0123456789
@&/?!%#'`""
[*+-=·::.,_]

project
High Grade Design Font,
editorial design, MdN
Corporation

country
Japan

year
2007

design
Happy & Happy, Inc.

team
Hajime Kabutoya

PROJECT
The Handbook on
Successful Ageing, *annual
report*, Tsao Foundation

COUNTRY
Singapore

YEAR
2009

DESIGN
Epigram

TEAM
Creative Director:
Edmund Wee
Design Director:
Yingser Chu
Project Manager:
Sokying Lo
Illustration:
Michelle Wan,
Stephanie Wong

PROJECT
I want the title of this book
to be, *book cover*, H55

COUNTRY
Singapore

YEAR
2001

DESIGN
H55

TEAM
Creative Director:
Hanson Ho

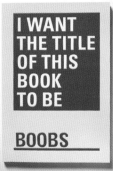

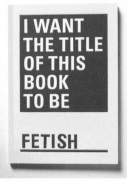

PROJECT

Snore Louder If You Can,
book design, Heman
Chong

COUNTRY

Singapore

YEAR

2006

DESIGN

H55

TEAM

Creative Director:
Hanson Ho

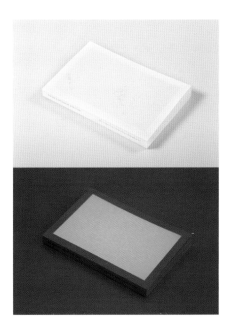

 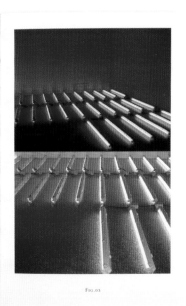

FIG.02

FIG.03

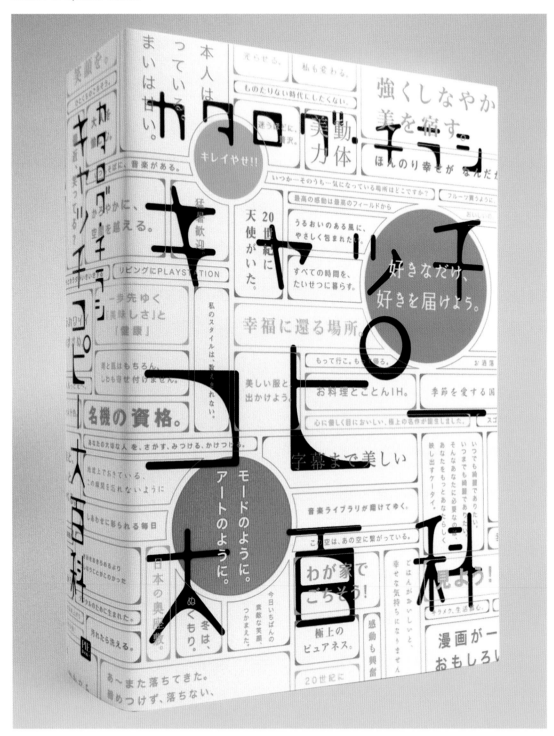

PROJECT
Slogan Encyclopedia, *book design*, Pie Books

COUNTRY
Japan

YEAR
2008

DESIGN
Happy & Happy, Inc.

TEAM
Hajime Kabutoya

PROJECT
Archigram: Experimental Architecture 1961–1974, *book design*, Art Tower Mito

COUNTRY
Japan

YEAR
2005

DESIGN
FLAME Inc.

TEAM
Art Direction/Design: Masayoshi Kodaira

PROJECT
President*s Design Award,
branding and book design,
Design Singapore Council

COUNTRY
Singapore

YEAR
2007

DESIGN
Black Design

TEAM
Jackson Tan

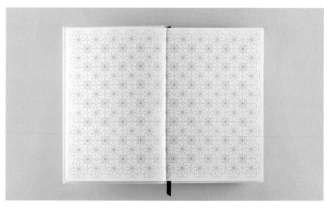

PROJECT
Typography in
Wonderland, *editorial
design*, Hongdesign Young
Designers' Exhibition

COUNTRY
South Korea

YEAR
2008

DESIGN
Minsun Eo

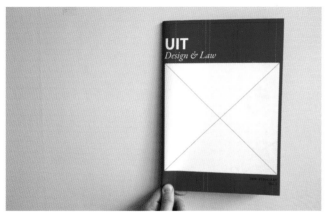

PROJECT
UIT Design & Law, *editorial design*, Kookmin University Law School

COUNTRY
South Korea

YEAR
2008

DESIGN
Heesun Seo

TEAM
Heesun Seo
Bora Kim

Maria Magdalena
Campos-Pons

Everything is Separated
by Water

PROJECT
Everything Is Separated By
Water, *catalogue design*,
Maria Magdalena
Campos-Pons

YEAR
2008

DESIGN
Ishan Khosla Design

COUNTRY
India

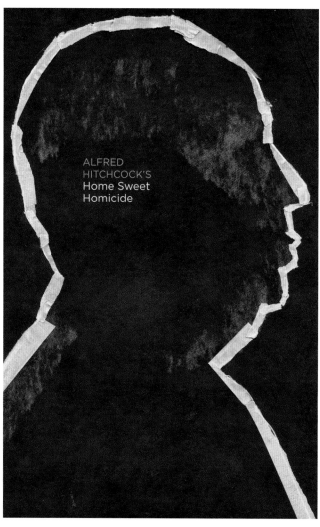

ALFRED
HITCHCOCK'S
Home Sweet
Homicide

ALFRED
HITCHCOCK'S
Most Wanted:
The First Lineup

PROJECT
Alfred Hitchcock, *book cover series*

COUNTRY
India

YEAR
2007

DESIGN
Ishan Khosla Design

ALFRED
HITCHCOCK'S
The Shadow
of Silence

ALFRED
HITCHCOCK'S
Tales of the
Supernatural
and Fantastic

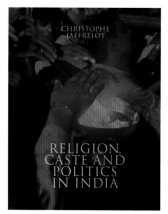
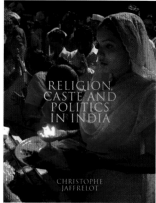
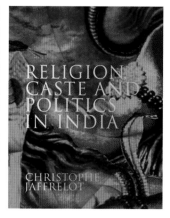
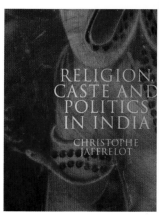

project
Religion,Caste and Politics
in India, *book covers series*,
Christophe Jaffrelot

country
India

year
2008

design
Ishan Khosla Design

The Man Whose Name did not Appear in the Census   Lajwanti

PROJECT
Mulk Raj Anand Series,
book cover series

COUNTRY
India

YEAR
2009

DESIGN
Ishan Khosla Design

Lament on the Death of a Master of the Arts   The Lost Child   Things Have a Way of Working Out

PROJECT
Baulsphere, *book cover,*
Mimlu Sem

COUNTRY
India

YEAR
2009

DESIGN
Ishan Khosla Design

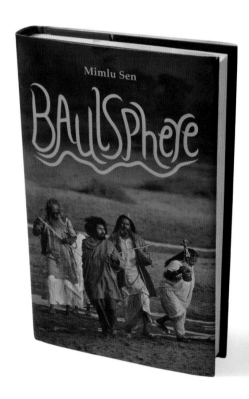

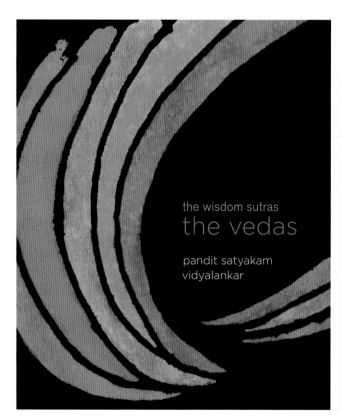

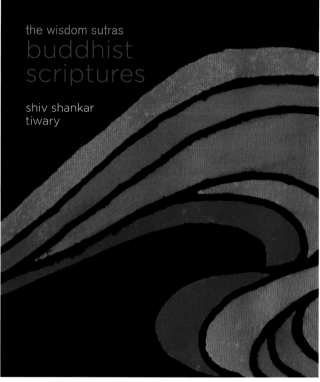

PROJECT
The Adventures of the
Missing Dancing Girl, *book
cover*, Sunila Gupte

COUNTRY
India

YEAR
2009

DESIGN
Ishan Khosla Design

PROJECT
The Wisdom Sutras
"The Vedas" and
"Buddhist Scriptures",
book cover series, Pandit
Satyakam Vidyalankar

COUNTRY
India

YEAR
2009

DESIGN
Ishan Khosla Design

平野啓一郎 ドーン

DAWN
Keiichiro Hirano

PROJECT
Dawn, *book cover*,
Keiichiro Hirano

COUNTRY
Japan

YEAR
2008

DESIGN
FLAME Inc.

TEAM
Art Direction/Design:
Masayoshi Kodaira

PROJECT
The Betelnut Killers, *book
cover*, Manisha Lakhe

COUNTRY
India

YEAR
2009

DESIGN
Ishan Khosla Design

PROJECT

The God Market, *book cover*, B.R. Nanda

COUNTRY

India

YEAR

2009

DESIGN

Ishan Khosla Design

PROJECT

The Road To Pakistan, *book cover*, B.R. Nanda

COUNTRY

India

YEAR

2009

DESIGN

Ishan Khosla Design

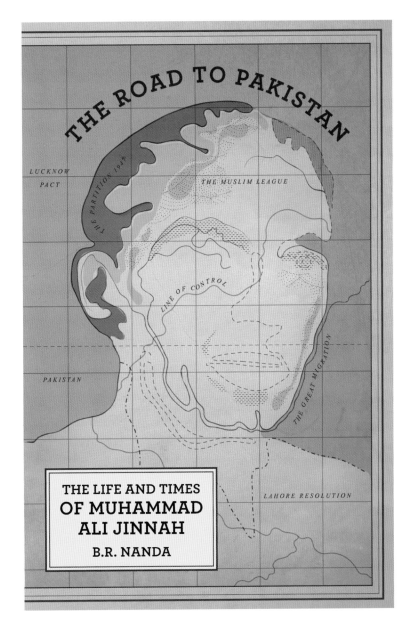

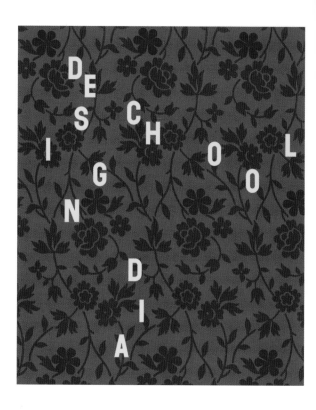

Project
Design School India,
book design

Country
India

Year
2005

Design
Ishan Khosla Design

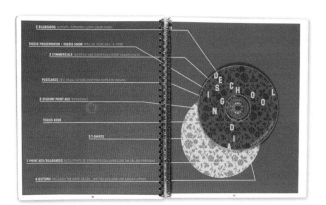

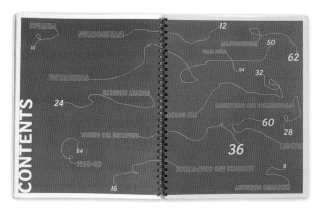

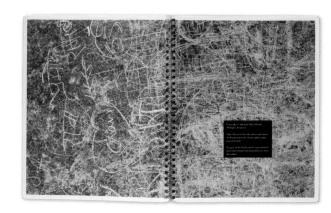

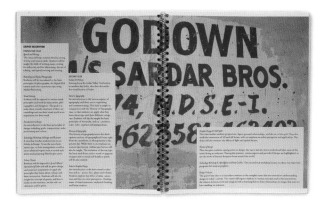

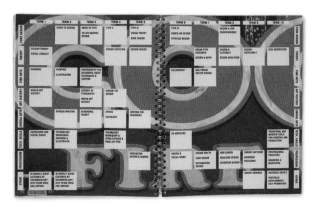

PROJECT
Geometry of Error, *book design*, Gallery Espace

COUNTRY
India

YEAR
2009

DESIGN
Ishan Khosla Design

PROJECT

Colour Cadences, *book design*, Kishor Shinde

COUNTRY

India

YEAR

2009

DESIGN

Ishan Khosla Design

colour cadences
KISHOR SHINDE

PROJECT
Code (Type) 1, *book design*, personal work

COUNTRY
South Korea

YEAR
2008

DESIGN
Jae-Hyouk Sung

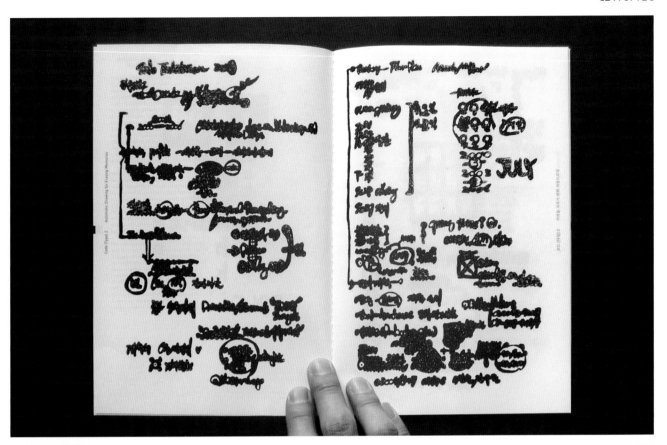

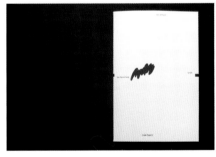

PROJECT
Code (Type) 2, *book design*, personal work

COUNTRY
South Korea

YEAR
2009

DESIGN
Jae-Hyouk Sung

PROJECT

A Chirstmas Cake!,
book design, Q-pot baby

COUNTRY

Japan

YEAR

2007

DESIGN

Rezon/Kawamura Hideo
Activity Inc.

TEAM

Creative Director/Design/
Illustration:
Hideo Kawamura
Design:
Tadaaki Wakamatsu
Writer:
Hiroyuki Aihara
Stylist:
Miki Aizawa
Photographer:
Fumiko Shibata
Hair Make:
Fusae Tachibana
Print:
Tenprint

PROJECT
Home Magazine, *magazine design*, X-Knowledge

COUNTRY
Japan

YEAR
2003

DESIGN
FLAME Inc.

PROJECT
Good Design, *catalogue design*, Japan Industrial Design Promotion Organization

COUNTRY
Japan

YEAR
2002–2003

DESIGN
FLAME Inc.

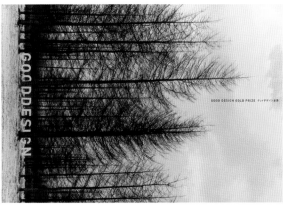

project
Sur | FACE, *booklet and DVD packaging*, UPLINK

country
Japan

year
2008

design
FLAME Inc.

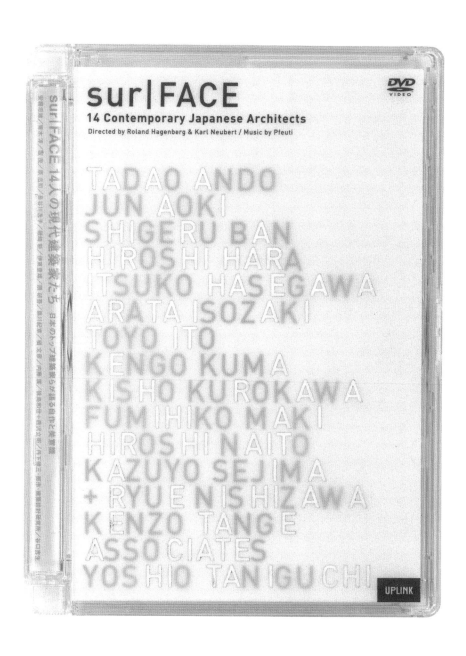

PROJECT
Landscape of Architectures,
booklet and DVD
packaging series, UPLINK

COUNTRY
Japan

YEAR
2009

DESIGN
FLAME Inc.

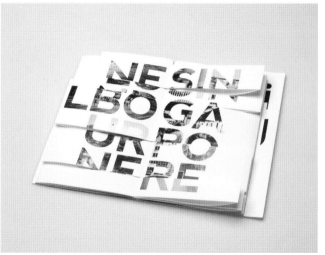
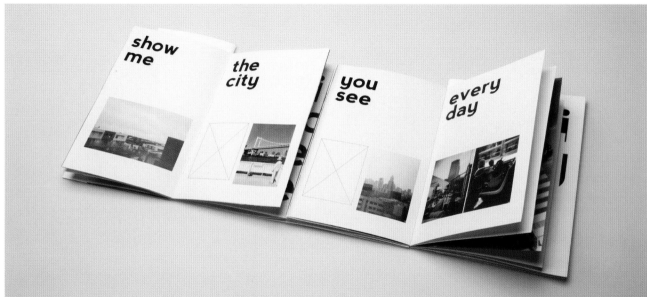
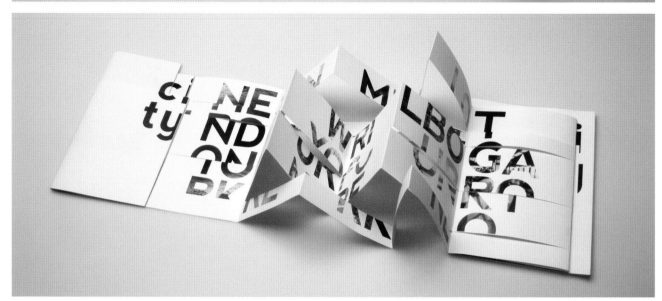

PROJECT
Untitled (city), *editorial
design*, personal work

COUNTRY
Singapore

YEAR
2009

DESIGN
May Chiang

TEAM
Photography:
Maho, George Lee

PROJECT
City Phenomena, *editorial
design*, personal work

COUNTRY
Singapore

YEAR
2009

DESIGN
May Chiang

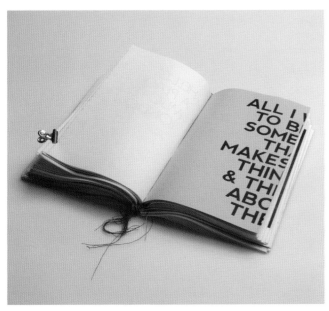

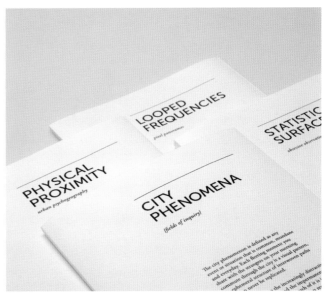

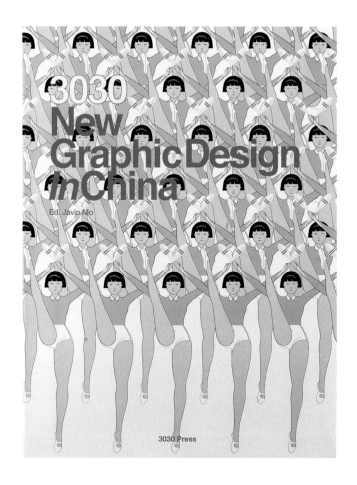

PROJECT
3030: New Graphic Design
in China, *book design*,
3030 Press

COUNTRY
Hong Kong/China

YEAR
2008

DESIGN
Milkxhake

TEAM
Jarvin Mo

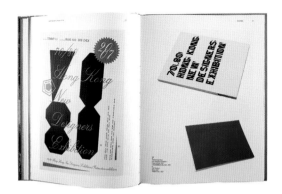

ISBN 978-988-99384-1-3

www.3030press.com

SD-06

SSH Utrecht /
馬德勒支 SSH
(2005)

PROJECT
Design 360° Concept
& Design Magazine,
magazine design, Sandu
Publishing Co., Ltd.

COUNTRY
Hong Kong/China

YEAR
2009

DESIGN
Milkxhake

TEAM
Jarvin Mo, Jan Cheung

/
360°F
FEATURE:

STOCKHOLM
DESIGN
LAB
訪談：SDL
/

- FEATURE -
訪談

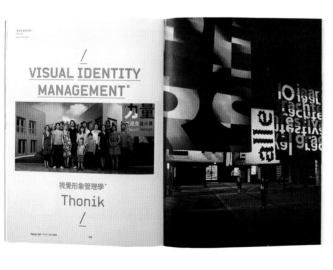

Project
Design 360° Concept
& Design Magazine,
magazine covers, Sandu
Publishing Co., Ltd.

Country
Hong Kong/China

Year
2009

Design
Milkxhake

Team
Jarvin Mo, Jan Cheung

PROJECT

Design 360° Concept
& Design Magazine,
magazine design, Sandu
Publishing Co., Ltd.

COUNTRY

Hong Kong/China

YEAR

2009

DESIGN

Milkxhake

TEAM

Jarvin Mo, Jan Cheung

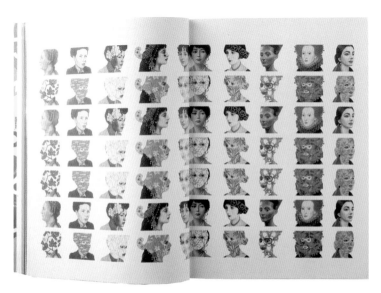

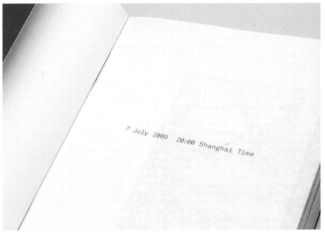

PROJECT
Facebook, *editorial and book design*, personal work

COUNTRY
China

YEAR
2009

DESIGN
Nelson Ng

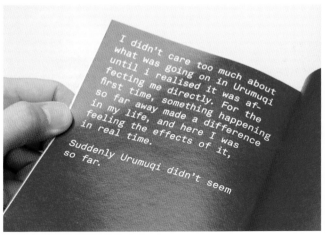

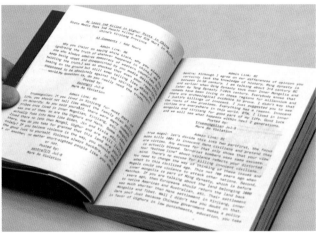

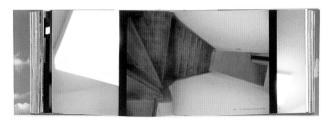

PROJECT
601 Space Project,
book design

COUNTRY
South Korea

YEAR
2003

DESIGN
601bisang

TEAM
Art Direction/Design:
Kum-jun Park
Design:
Seung-youn Nam, Seol Kim

PROJECT
True Colors, *catalogue*,
Fuchu Art Museum

COUNTRY
Japan

YEAR
2008

DESIGN
Nakano Design Office

TEAM
Takeo Nakano,
Tsutomu Mutoh

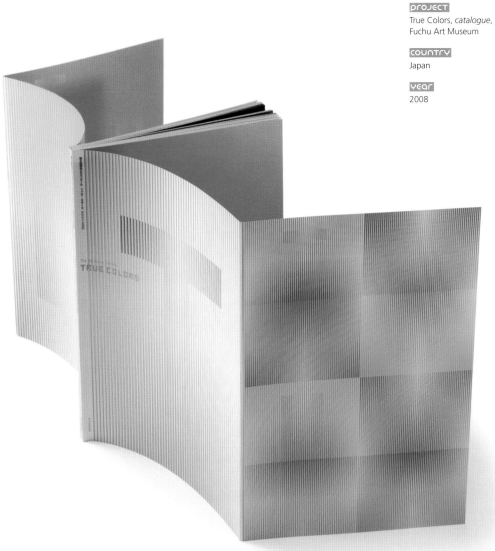

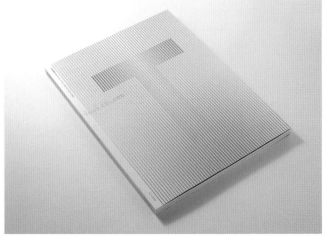

PROJECT
Prototype Exhibition 02,
catalogue, Prototype
Exhibition Executive
Committee

COUNTRY
Japan

YEAR
2008

DESIGN
Nakano Design Office

TEAM
Takeo Nakano

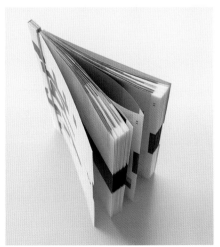

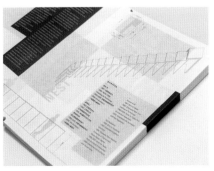

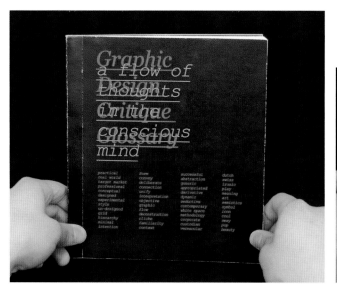

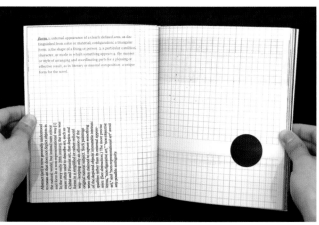

PROJECT
Graphic Design Critique
Glossary, *book design*,
Personal work

COUNTRY
China

YEAR
2008

DESIGN
Nelson Ng

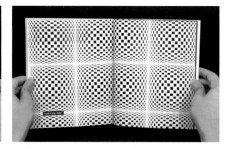

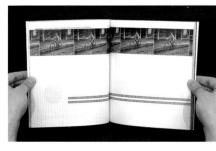

DOT.LINE

デザイン・アイデア素材集／ドット・ライン
Designed and Produced by SLOW inc.

WORKS CORPORATION

Dot_Circle_
Dot_Square_
Dot_Triangle_
Dot_Geometry_
Line_
Grid_
Geometry_

ドット・ラブ。

デザインワークが加速する。使えるグラフィックリソース集

PROJECT
DOT.LINE, *editorial design*, SLOW inc.

COUNTRY
Japan

YEAR
2008

DESIGN
SLOW Inc.

TEAM
Daisuke Hara

PROJECT
New Graphic Magazine
China, *magazine design*

COUNTRY
China

YEAR
2004–2010

DESIGN
Seecoo Studio

TEAM
Editor in chief:
Ge Hong
Sub-editor:
Jiang Jie
Executive Editor:
Li Dawei, Wang Jing
Art Editor:
Chen Yang, Hua Pei,
Kan Wenkang,
Yang Jiefang

PROJECT
Design&Life Online
Magazine, *magazine
and editorial design*

COUNTRY
Taiwan/China

YEAR
2007

DESIGN
PHDC

TEAM
Po-hsuan Hsu,
Yin-wen Chen

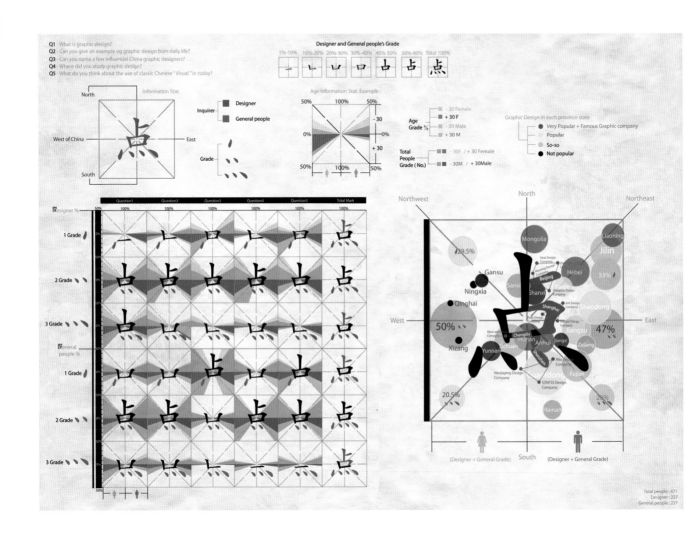

PROJECT
What is Graphic Design?,
*editorial information
graphic*, personal work

COUNTRY
China

YEAR
2008

DESIGN
Cheng Qingqing

PROJECT

Such Treasure and Rich
Merchandize, *catalogue*,
NCBS, The National
Institute of Biological
Sciences

COUNTRY

India

YEAR

2008

DESIGN

Trapeze

TEAM

Sarita Sundar, Ram Sinam,
Aparna Ranjan, Georgie
Paul, Sybil Rodrigues,
Aditi Dilip

PROJECT
Free type covers,
personal work

COUNTRY
Thailand

YEAR
2009

DESIGN
TNOP Design

TEAM
Tnop Wangsillapakun

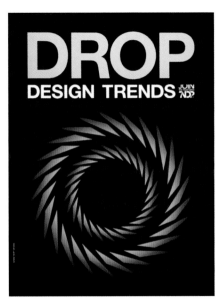

PROJECT
CGWORLD, *magazine design*, Works Corporation

COUNTRY
Japan

YEAR
2009

DESIGN
SLOW Inc.

TEAM
Hara Daisuke

project
Phaneng, *editorial design*, S. Jodha

country
India

year
2008

design
Trapeze

team
Ram Sinam

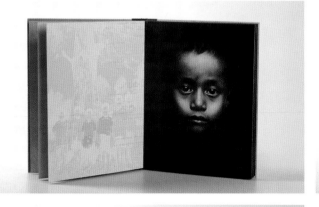

PROJECT
Phaneng, *postcards set*,
S. Jodha

COUNTRY
India

YEAR
2009

DESIGN
Trapeze

TEAM
Ram Sinam,
Sybil Rodrigues

PROJECT
Soak, *book design*,
Anuradha Mathur &
Dilip da Cunha

COUNTRY
India

YEAR
2009

DESIGN
Trapeze

TEAM
Ram Sinam,
Aparna Ranjan

PROJECT
Werk magazine,
magazine design, Werk

COUNTRY
Singapore

YEAR
2010

DESIGN
Work

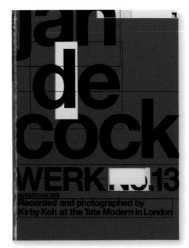

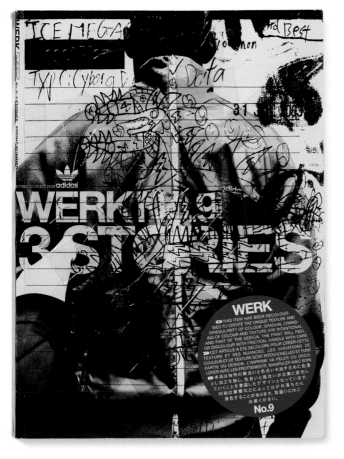

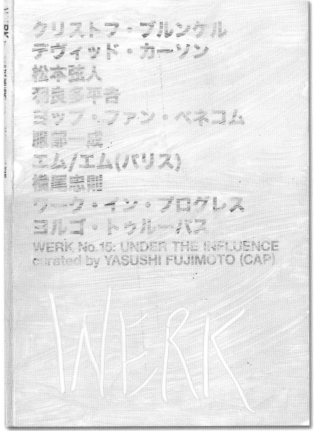

PROJECT
Club21 magazine,
magazine design, Club21

COUNTRY
Singapore

YEAR
2009

DESIGN
Work

PROJECT
W+K Book III,
editorial design

COUNTRY
China

YEAR
2009

DESIGN
Wieden + Kennedy
Shanghai

TEAM
Art Director:
Dong Wei
Copywriter:
Roberto Danino, Zebra Hua
Designer:
Driv Loo, Sally Zou
Digital Creative:
Francis Lam, Leal Bao
Production:
Vic Zhang, Stone Xue

Photography:
Wieden + Kennedy
Printing Binding:
Shanghai Jingyang Color
Printing Ltd.
USB Rabbit collaborated
with Super Nature Design

letni

non-
commercial

PROJECT
Picnic Calendar, *greeting card calendar*, D-Bros

COUNTRY
Japan

YEAR
2008

DESIGN
10 Inc.

TEAM
Masahiro Kakinokihara

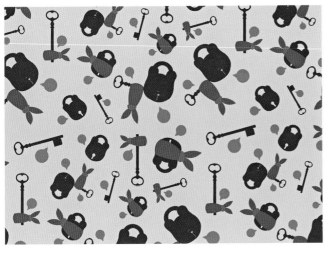
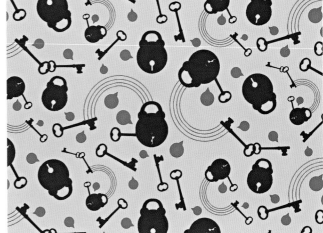

PROJECT
Made Up, *gridwork graphics*

COUNTRY
China

YEAR
2009

DESIGN
Adeline Chua

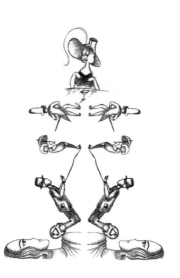

PROJECT
Ink In, *illustration*

COUNTRY
China

YEAR
2009

DESIGN
Adeline Chua

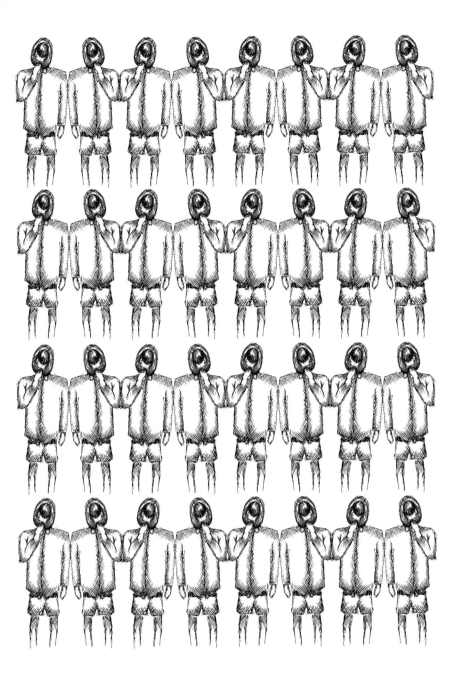

PROJECT
Made Up, *gridwork graphics*

COUNTRY
China

YEAR
2009

DESIGN
Adeline Chua

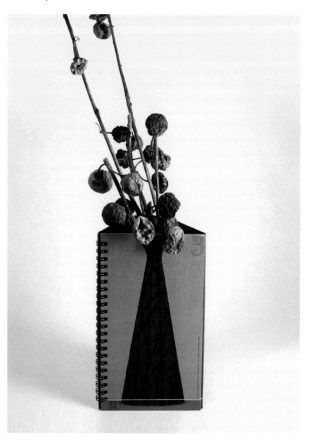

PROJECT
Calendar, Heiwa Paper

COUNTRY
Hong Kong/China

YEAR
2006

DESIGN
Ameba Design

TEAM
Gideon Lai, Kenji

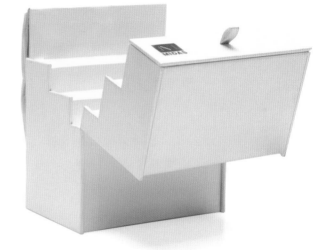

PROJECT
Calendar, Midas Group

COUNTRY
Hong Kong/China

YEAR
2006

DESIGN
Ameba Design

TEAM
Gideon Lai, Ray

PROJECT
ETIME, *booklet clock*
installation art,
personal work

COUNTRY
Hong Kong/China

YEAR
2007

DESIGN
Ameba Design

TEAM
Gideon Lai, Kenji, Vincent

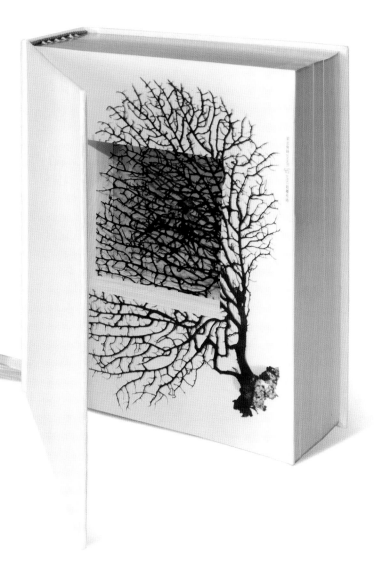

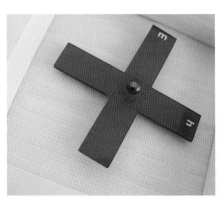

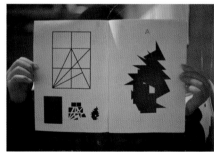

project
A4 Letters, *exhibition*

year
2009

country
South Korea

design
Goo-Ryong Kang

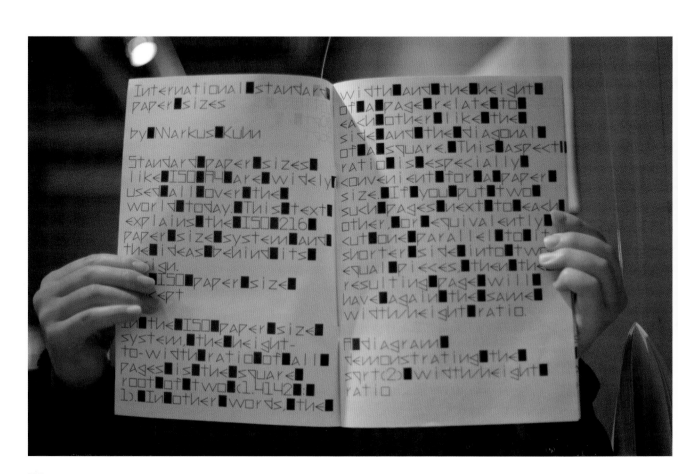

PROJECT
"&" Space (Gold Cross),
poster and installation art,
6 Said Show

COUNTRY
Hong Kong/China

YEAR
2007

DESIGN
Ameba Design

TEAM
Gideon Lai

PROJECT
Barbie Carpet,
carpet design, Matel

COUNTRY
China

YEAR
2009

DESIGN
Chen Hangfeng

PROJECT
Beautiful New World,
print, personal work

COUNTRY
China

YEAR
2008

DESIGN
Chen Hangfeng

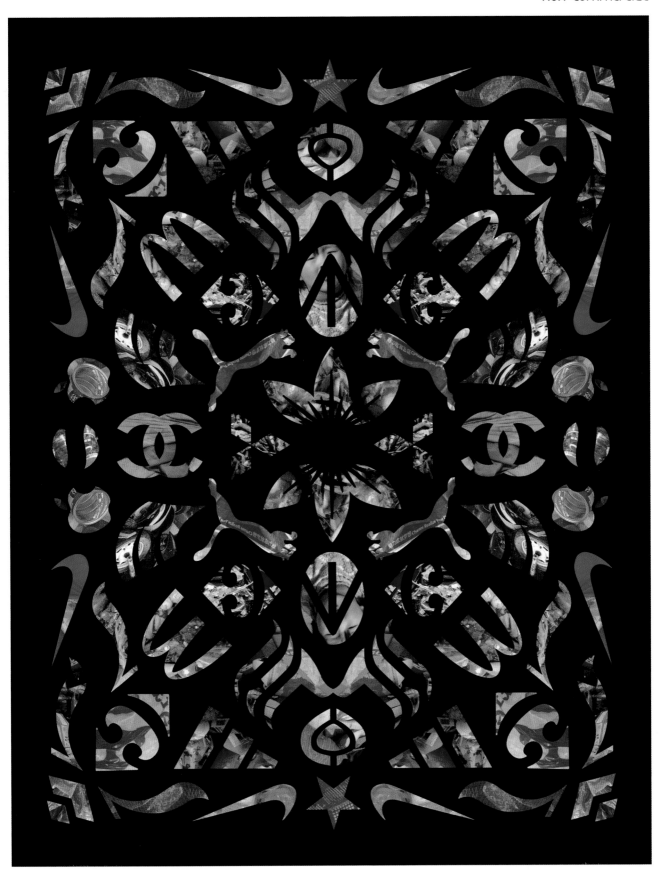

PROJECT
ChristMASS Production,
vinyl applied on window,
personal work

COUNTRY
China

YEAR
2008

DESIGN
Chen Hangfeng

PROJECT
China Chaos/ChinaChic,
wallpaper, personal work

COUNTRY
China

YEAR
2008

DESIGN
Chen Hangfeng

PROJECT
Logomania Brand City,
print, personal work

COUNTRY
China

YEAR
2008

DESIGN
Chen Hangfeng

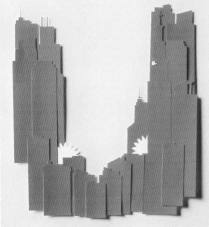

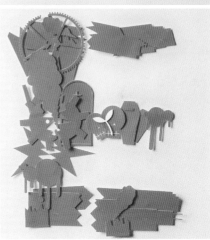

PROJECT
Read, *typeface*,
personal work

COUNTRY
South Korea

YEAR
2008

DESIGN
Hanuku

TEAM
Hwan uk Choe

PROJECT
Logomania Doudle
Happiness, *print*,
personal work

COUNTRY
China

YEAR
2008

DESIGN
Chen Hangfeng

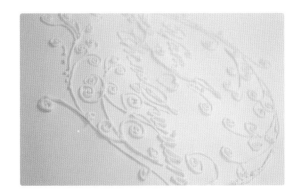
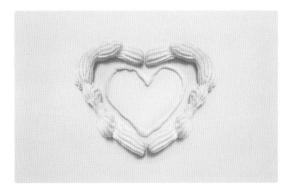

PROJECT
Cream Painting, *wedding invitation*, personal work

COUNTRY
China

YEAR
2009

DESIGN
Ling Meng

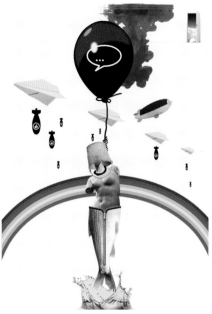

PROJECT
Elevate, *illustration*

COUNTRY
India

YEAR
2007–2009

DESIGN
dev kabir malik * design

TEAM
Dev Kabir Malik

project
Martin Venezky,
illustration, Old Dominion
University

country
South Korea

year
2009

design
Jiwon Lee

team
Aaron Michael Lambino,
Samantha McLenegan,
Shawn Staggs, Jiwon Lee

project
Hybridity, *illustration*,
personal work

country
South Korea

year
2005

design
Jiwon Lee

Visiting Artist Lecture
Martin Venezky
3/18 Wednesday 7 p.m.
Baron and Ellin Gordon Art Galleries

Poster Design Aaron Michael Lambino, Samantha McLenegan, Shawn Staggs, Gl Lee

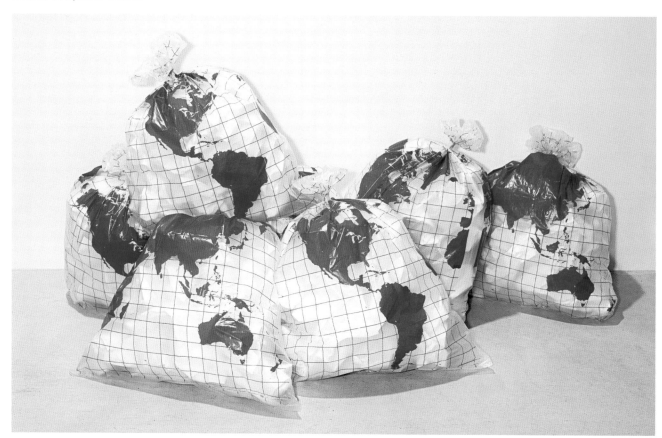

PROJECT
Trash Bag in the Earth,
Chikyu Gomi Bukuro

COUNTRY
Japan

YEAR
2009

DESIGN
MR_DESIGN

TEAM
Art Direction:
Kenjiro Sano
Design:
Yuko Endo

project
PIG MUG, *mug design*,
Franc Franc

country
Japan

year
2002

design
MR_DESIGN

team
Art Direction/Design:
Kenjiro Sano

PROJECT
Eco Warrior Bag High
Class, *illustration on bag*,
personal work

COUNTRY
Japan

YEAR
2007

DESIGN
Rezon/Kawamura Hideo
Activity Inc.

TEAM
Hideo Kawamura

PROJECT
ONOFF, *illustration*

COUNTRY
Japan

YEAR
2006

DESIGN
Rezon/Kawamura Hideo
Activity Inc.

TEAM
Hideo Kawamura

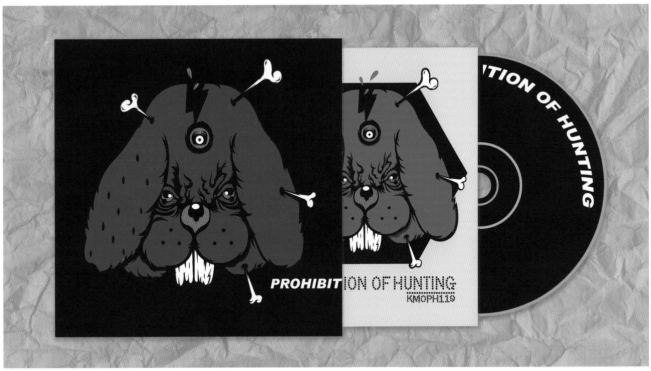

PROJECT
Care for the earth,
illustration, personal work

COUNTRY
China

YEAR
2001

DESIGN
Kzeng

PROJECT
The story about flowers,
illustration, personal work

COUNTRY
China

YEAR
2001

DESIGN
Kzeng

PROJECT
Billion Dollar Bloodbath,
print, personal work

COUNTRY
China

YEAR
2008

DESIGN
Kzeng

PROJECT
Dry Plant Book, *illustration*,
personal work

COUNTRY
China

YEAR
2009

DESIGN
Ling Meng

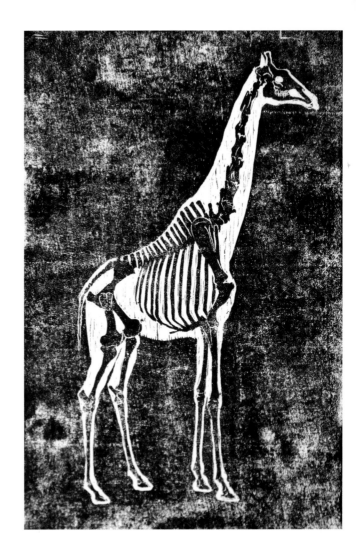

PROJECT
Fossil Giraffe, *prints*,
Personal work

COUNTRY
China

YEAR
2008

DESIGN
Ling Meng

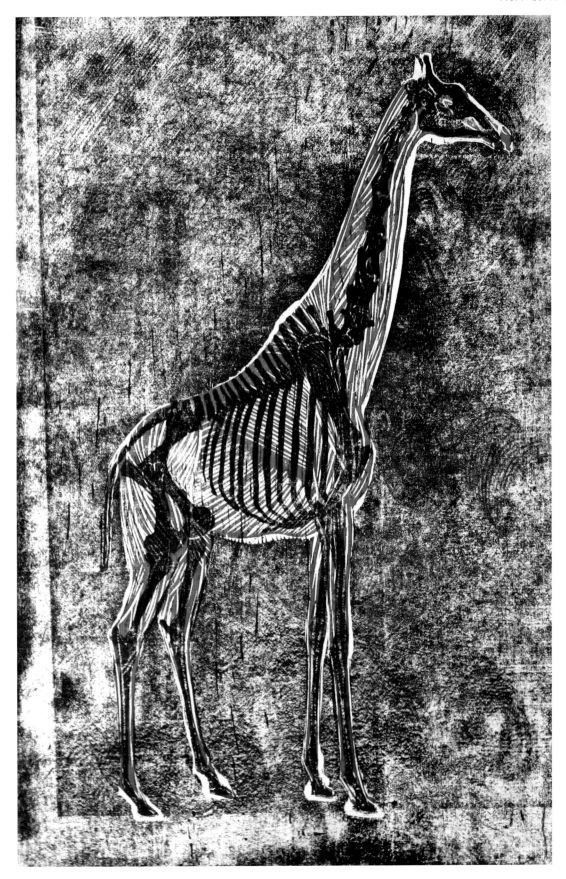

project
Old Newspaper, illustration,
personal work

country
China

year
2008

design
Ling Meng

PROJECT
Pig Flu, illustration,
personal work

COUNTRY
China

YEAR
2009

DESIGN
Ling Meng

PROJECT
Wieden + Kennedy
Window, *graphics*, Wieden
+ Kennedy Shanghai

COUNTRY
China

YEAR
2009

DESIGN
Momorobo

PROJECT
This City Was Never
Here, *project, poster,
typeface, book, T-shirt*,
personal work

COUNTRY
South Korea

YEAR
2009

DESIGN
Heesun Seo

TEAM
Heesun Seo, Eunsang Lee,
Hwan uk Choe

'THIS CITY WAS NEVER HERE'
by LSD (Esam Lee, Heesun Seo, Hwanuk Choe).

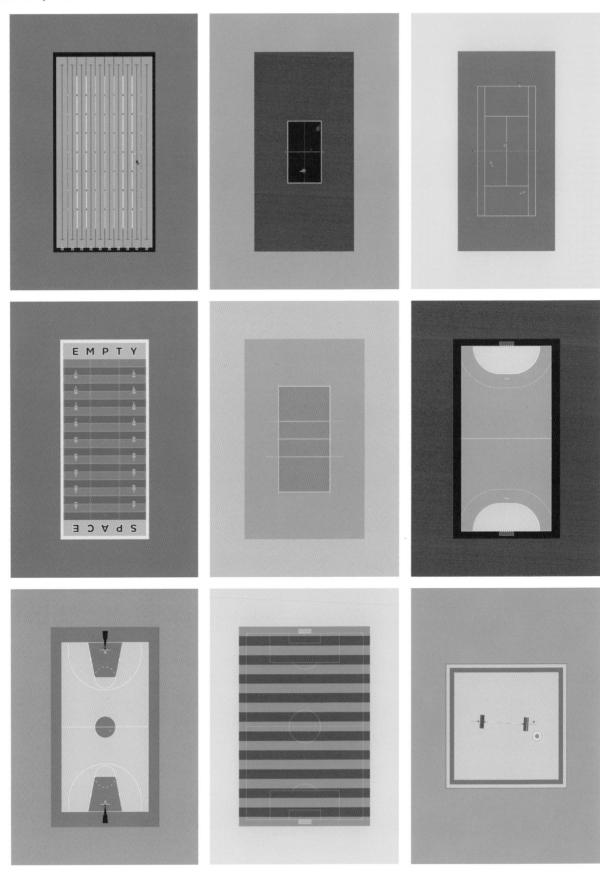

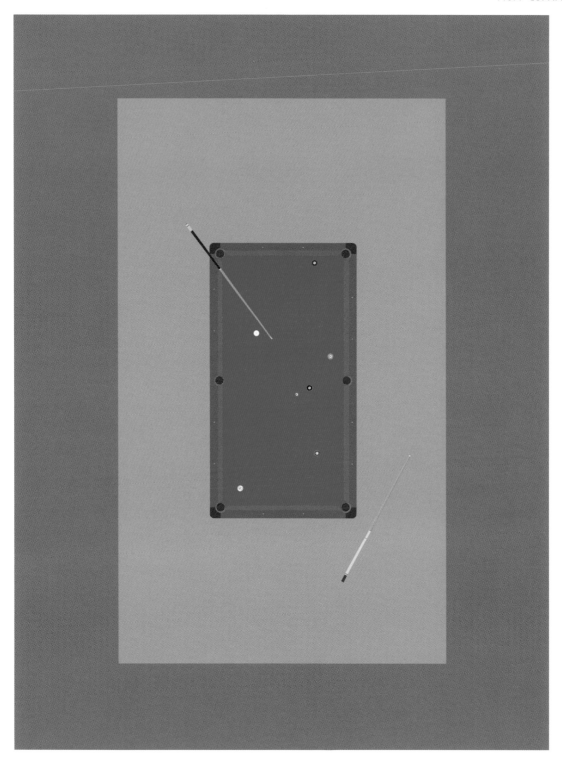

PROJECT
Empty Space, *illustration*,
personal work

COUNTRY
South Korea

YEAR
2008

DESIGN
Mulgunamu Studio

TEAM
Dongjoo Seo

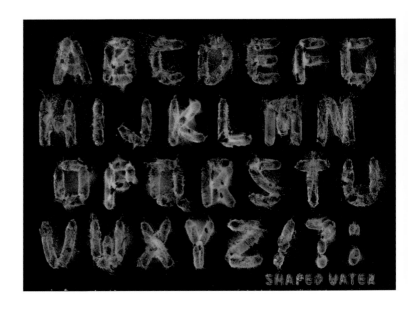

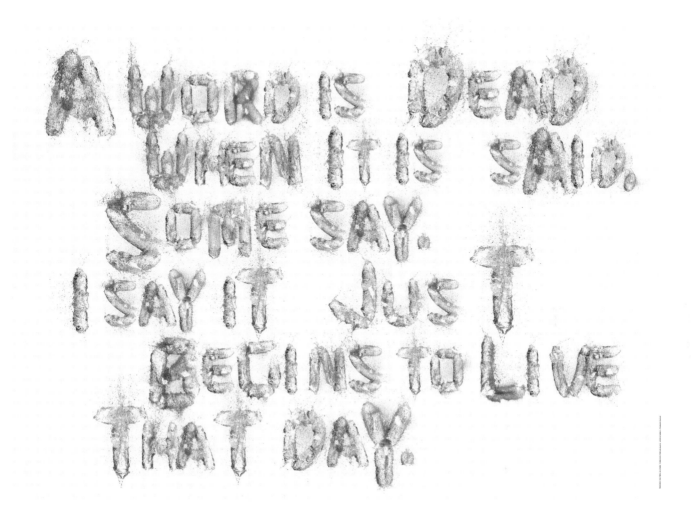

PROJECT
Shaped Water, *poster and typography*

COUNTRY
Japan

YEAR
2009

DESIGN
finch-talk

TEAM
Art Direction:
Nobuhiro Kobayashi
Poem:
Emily Dickinson

PROJECT
Kingashinnen 08,
new year card

COUNTRY
Japan

YEAR
2008

DESIGN
finch-talk

TEAM
Art Direction:
Nobuhiro Kobayashi

PROJECT
Big Mouth Cup, *exhibition
concept, design, graphics,
personal work*

COUNTRY
China

YEAR
2008

DESIGN
Pan Jianfeng

PROJECT
Bund 18, *exhibition
concept, design*,
personal work

COUNTRY
China

YEAR
2008

DESIGN
Pan Jianfeng

PROJECT

If Mao only knew,
exhibition concept,
graphics, personal work

COUNTRY

China

YEAR

2008

DESIGN

Pan Jianfeng

PROJECT

Little Thinking Man,
*exhibition concept,
graphics*, personal work

COUNTRY

China

YEAR

2007

DESIGN

Pan Jianfeng

PROJECT
Taku Satoh Exhibition
"3-D Hiragana",
exhibition

COUNTRY
Japan

YEAR
2009

DESIGN
Taku Satoh Design
Office Inc.

TEAM
Taku Satoh

PROJECT
Electricity, *illustration,*
personal work

COUNTRY
Singapore

YEAR
2008

DESIGN
Phunk Studio

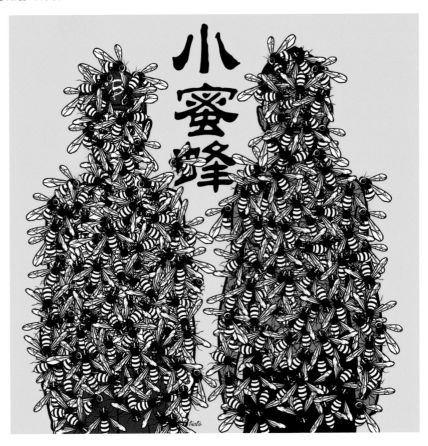

PROJECT
The Bees, *graphics*,
personal work

COUNTRY
Singapore

YEAR
2009

DESIGN
Phunk Studio

PROJECT
Art, *illustration*,
Time Out Hong Kong

COUNTRY
Singapore

YEAR
2009

DESIGN
Phunk Studio

PROJECT
2010=MMX, *illustration*,
personal work

COUNTRY
South Korea

YEAR
2010

DESIGN
Jae-Hyouk Sung

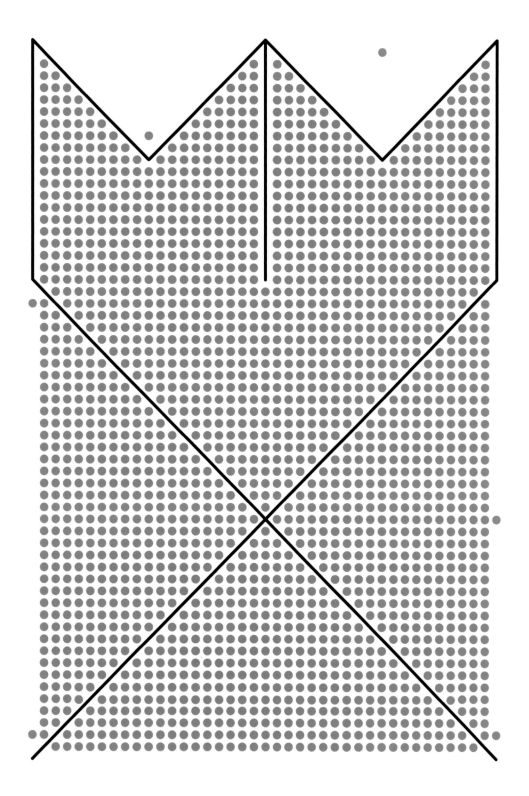

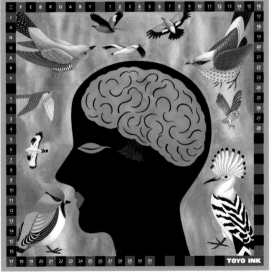

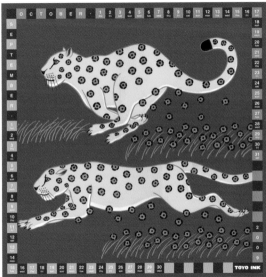

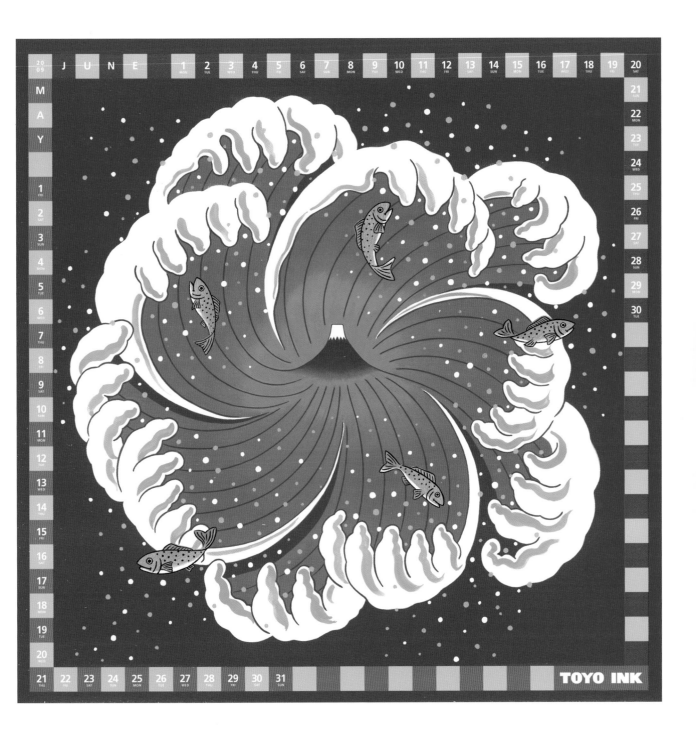

PROJECT
Illustrated calendar,
Toyo Ink

COUNTRY
Japan

YEAR
2010

DESIGN
Designfarm

TEAM
U.G. Sato

new

packaging

PROJECT
Killiney, *packaging set*

COUNTRY
Singapore

YEAR
2007

DESIGN
&Larry

TEAM
Creative Director/Designer:
Larry Peh

PROJECT
Chinese Tea Set,
packaging set

COUNTRY
Hong Kong/China

YEAR
2009

DESIGN
Ameba Design

TEAM
Gideo Lai

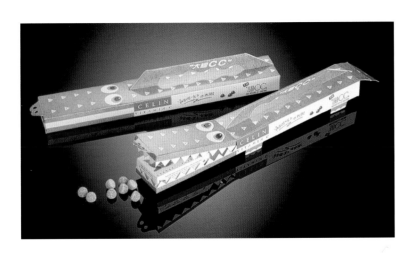

PROJECT
Celin Vitamin C,
promotional packaging

COUNTRY
Hong Kong/China

YEAR
2009

DESIGN
Ameba Design

TEAM
Gideo Lai

PROJECT
Kazu, *packaging*, Kazu
Jewelry Design Studio

COUNTRY
Japan

YEAR
1989

DESIGN
Akio Okumura

PCI envelope, *packaging*,
Packing Create Inc.

Japan

1998

Akio Okumura

PROJECT
Keystar, *branding and packaging set*

COUNTRY
Hong Kong/China

YEAR
2009

DESIGN
Ameba Design

TEAM
Gideon Lai, Vincent, Kenji

PROJECT
Flower Tea, *packaging set*,
Yu Ming

COUNTRY
Hong Kong/China

YEAR
2007

DESIGN
Ameba Design

TEAM
Gideo Lai

PROJECT
Nesvita, *packaging set*,
Nestlé

COUNTRY
Hong Kong/China

YEAR
2009

DESIGN
Ameba Design

TEAM
Gideo Lai

PROJECT
3302 Enviroment Paper
Swatch, *paper swatch*,
Heiwa Paper

COUNTRY
Hong Kong/China

YEAR
2008

DESIGN
Ameba Design

TEAM
Gideo Lai, Kenson

PROJECT
Heiwa Paper Swatch /
5 Lights & 10 Colours,
swatch book, Heiwa Paper

COUNTRY
Hong Kong/China

YEAR
2009

DESIGN
Ameba Design

TEAM
Gideo Lai, Kenji

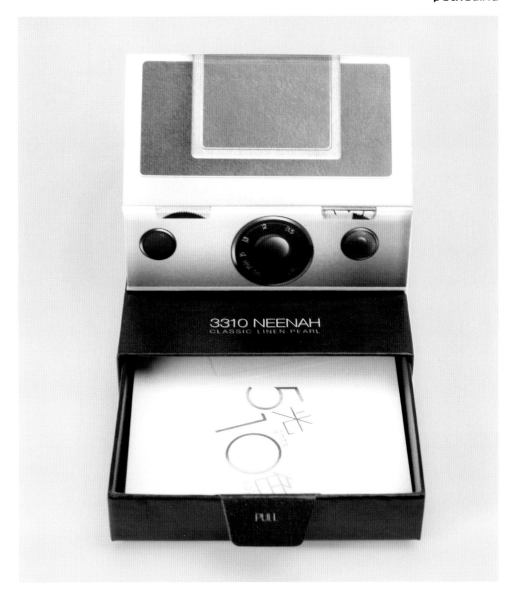

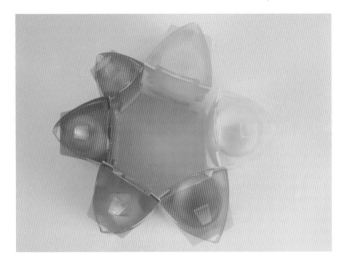

PROJECT
Lamps, *packaging set*,
graduation project

COUNTRY
China

YEAR
2009

DESIGN
JC Studio

TEAM
Jimmy Zhao

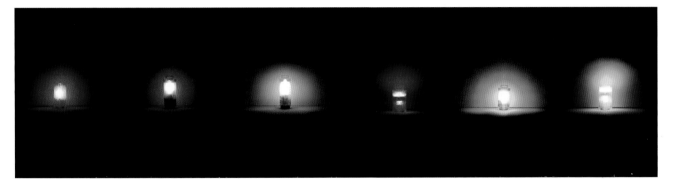

PROJECT
Ninki Ichi / Junmai Ginjo
Sake, *bottle and external
packaging*, Daiginjo

COUNTRY
Japan

YEAR
2009

DESIGN
10 Inc.

その酒、しゅわと来ませり。

発泡吟醸酒［美丈夫しゅわっ!!］

project

Bijofu Schwa, *packaging, poster and advertising*, Hamakawa Brewery Co., Ltd.

country

Japan

year

2006

design

office m

team

Design:
Mihoko Hachiuma
Copy:
Akemi Ikeda
Photography:
Nobuyoshi Kawakami

PROJECT
Dissolu tea, *packaging*,
Lao Tsu Say Enterprise Ltd.

COUNTRY
Taiwan/China

YEAR
2008

DESIGN
Leslie Chan Design
Co., Ltd.

TEAM
Leslie Chan Wing Kei

PROJECT
Rosier, *packaging*

COUNTRY
Japan

YEAR
2008

DESIGN
iyamadesign inc.

TEAM
Koji Iyama

PROJECT
Meizhou Mazu Water,
packaging, Mariana
Biotech Co., Ltd

COUNTRY
Taiwan/China

YEAR
2008

DESIGN
Leslie Chan Design
Co., Ltd.

TEAM
Leslie Chan Wing Kei

PROJECT

12 Months in a Yuzu Citrus
Farm, *packaging and
leaflet*, Ikeda-Yugaen

COUNTRY

Japan

YEAR

2008–2009

DESIGN

office m

TEAM

Design:
Mihoko Hachiuma
Copy:
Akemi Ikeda
Photography:
Nobuyoshi Kawakami

PROJECT
Neige, *packaging*,
Confectionery Goto

COUNTRY
Japan

YEAR
2004

DESIGN
office m

TEAM
Mihoko Hachiuma

PROJECT
Japon Tomato Ketchup,
packaging, Kensho Co.,
Ltd.

COUNTRY
Japan

YEAR
2009

DESIGN
office m

TEAM
Mihoko Hachiuma

PROJECT
Kojun Japan, *packaging set*, Kojun Japan Co., Ltd.

COUNTRY
Japan

YEAR
2006–2008

DESIGN
Romando Co., Ltd.

TEAM
Art Direction:
Miyauchi Kenji
Design:
Imada Misa
Creative Director:
Kamada Takashi
Producer:
Kuragaki Tomohiko
Copy:
Ito Satoshi, Takahashi Rei,
Takeda Kiyomi

PROJECT
Imoya Kinjiro, *packaging and advertising*, Shibuya Foods Co., Ltd.

COUNTRY
Japan

YEAR
2005

DESIGN
office m

TEAM
Design:
Mihoko Hachiuma
Copy:
Akemi Ikeda
Photography:
Nobuyoshi Kawakami

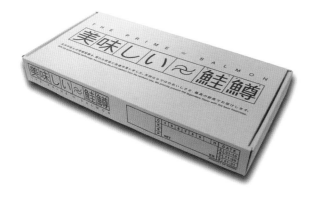

PROJECT
S Road, *packaging set*,
S Road Co., Ltd

COUNTRY
Japan

YEAR
2005–2009

DESIGN
Romando Co., Ltd.

TEAM
Art Direction:
Simon Browning
Designer:
Murata Kyoichiro
Creative Director:
Kamada Takashi
Producer:
Kubota Masashi
Copy:
Takahashi Rei,
Tamura Madoka

PROJECT
Hi No Ka, *packaging set, brochure and advertising,* Matsusaki Frozen Dessert Industries, Ltd.

COUNTRY
Japan

YEAR
2006–2009

DESIGN
office m

TEAM
Design:
Mihoko Hachiuma
Copy:
Akemi Ikeda
Photography:
Nobuyoshi Kawakami

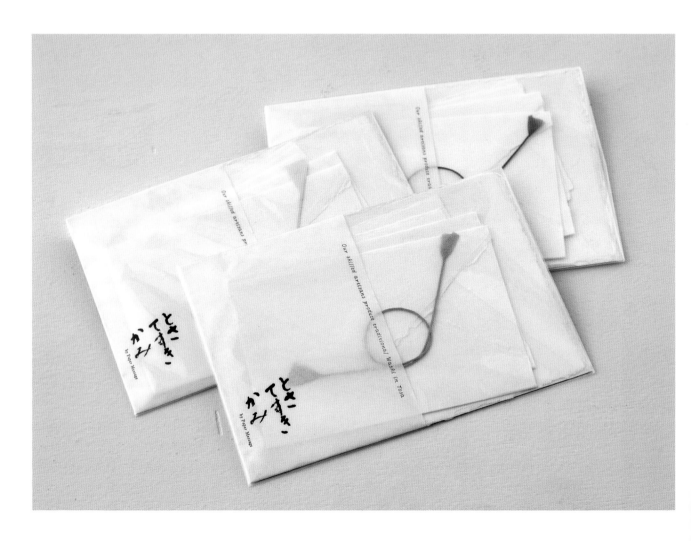

PROJECT
Letter Set of Tosa Washi,
packaging, Paper Message

COUNTRY
Japan

YEAR
2005

DESIGN
office m

TEAM
Mihoko Hachiuma

PROJECT
Wasanbon, *packaging*,
Isuzu-chaya

COUNTRY
Japan

YEAR
2004

DESIGN
office m

TEAM
Mihoko Hachiuma

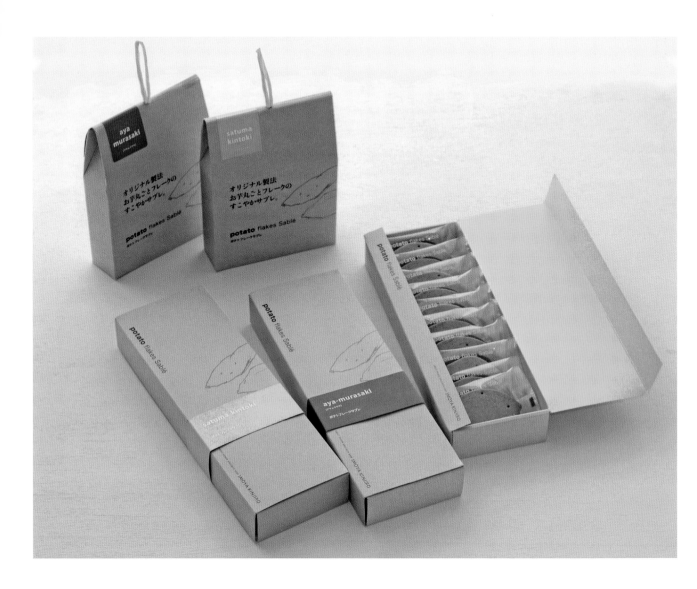

PROJECT
potato flakes Sable,
packaging set, Shibuya
Foods Co., Ltd

COUNTRY
Japan

YEAR
2005

DESIGN
office m

TEAM
Mihoko Hachiuma

PROJECT
boite de bijou, *corporate identity, packaging set*, boite de bijou pâtisserie

COUNTRY
Taiwan/China

YEAR
2006

DESIGN
PHDC

TEAM
Po-hsuan Hsu, Yin-wen Chen

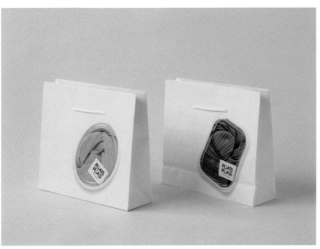
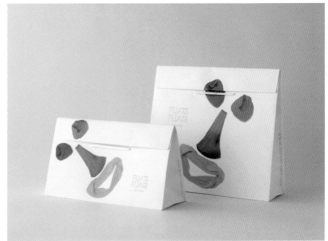

PROJECT
Issey Miyake Pleats Please,
packaging set, Issey
Miyake Inc.

COUNTRY
Japan

YEAR
2005

DESIGN
Taku Satoh Design
Office Inc.

TEAM
Taku Satoh

PROJECT
Q-CUP Instant Noodle,
packaging, Wei Chuan
Foods Corporation

COUNTRY
Taiwan/China

YEAR
2006

DESIGN
Leslie Chan Design
Co., Ltd.

TEAM
Leslie Chan Wing Kei

PROJECT
Odeur 71, *packaging and advertising*, Comme des Garçons

COUNTRY
Japan

YEAR
2009

DESIGN
FLAME Inc.,
E.P.A.

TEAM
Masayoshi kodaira

PROJECT
Tea Bag, *packaging*

COUNTRY
Japan

YEAR
2009

DESIGN
Cross Chrome

TEAM
Hitoshi Okazaki,
Rie Amaki

PROJECT
Nothing else but tea,
packaging, Lao Tsu Say
Enterprise Ltd.

COUNTRY
Taiwan/China

YEAR
2008

DESIGN
Leslie Chan Design
Co., Ltd.

TEAM
Leslie Chan Wing Kei

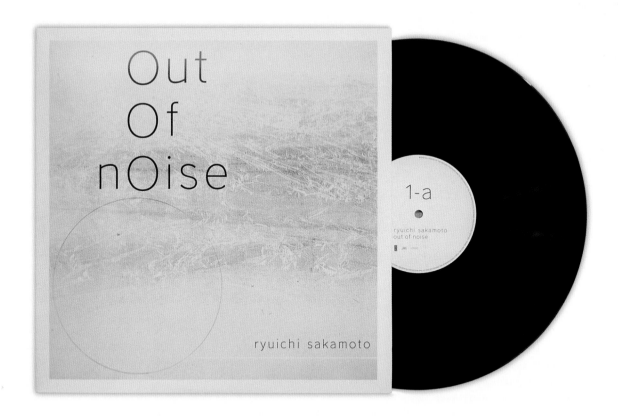

project

Out of noise, *Record packaging and tour book*, Ryuichi Sakamoto, Commmons

country

Japan

year

2009

design

Nakajima Design

team

Hideki Nakajima

PROJECT
Akiko Yano, CD
package, Yamaha Music
Communications

COUNTRY
Japan

YEAR
2006

DESIGN
Bluemark Inc.

TEAM
Art Direction/Design:
Atsuki Kikuchi

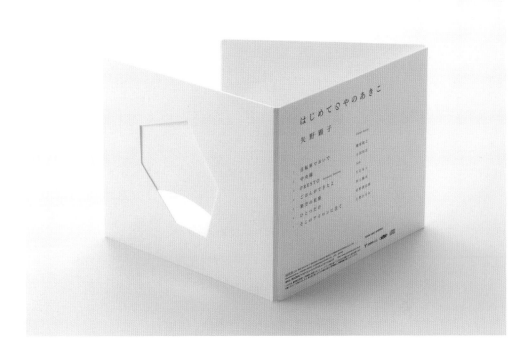

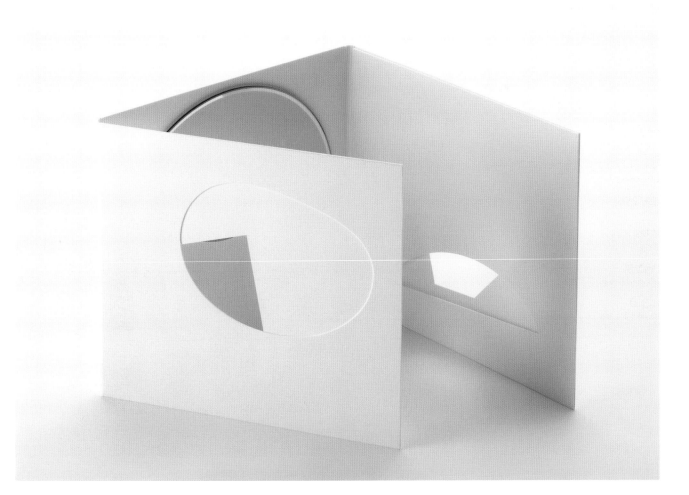

project
COMPLEX / No? Yes!!,
CD package, Rock Chipper
Record Co., Ltd.

country
Japan

year
2003

design
ALFAEYES design Inc.

team
Design:
Yoshie Yokoyama
Photography:
Hisayoshi Osawa

project
Engawa-Space / Bamboo
Shigeru, *CD package*,
Rock Chipper Record
Co., Ltd.

country
Japan

year
2003

design
ALFAEYES design Inc.

team
Design:
Yoshie Yokoyama
Photography:
Hisayoshi Osawa

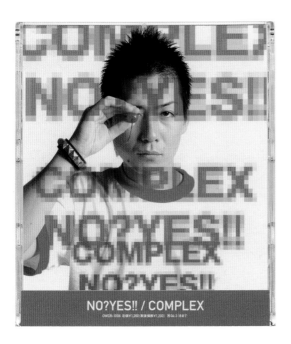

PROJECT
Crossroad / No? Yes!!,
CD package, Rock Chipper
Record Co., Ltd.

COUNTRY
Japan

YEAR
2003

DESIGN
ALFAEYES design Inc.

TEAM
Design:
Yoshie Yokoyama
Photography:
Kenji Onuma

PROJECT
Future / ILLUMINA,
CD package,
Pony Canyon Inc.

COUNTRY
Japan

YEAR
2002

DESIGN
ALFAEYES design Inc.

TEAM
Design:
Yoshie Yokoyama
Photography:
Hideo Kanno

PROJECT

Some probability of one half billion / ILLUMINA, *CD package*, Pony Canyon Inc.

COUNTRY

Japan

YEAR

2002

DESIGN

ALFAEYES design Inc.

TEAM

Design:
Yoshie Yokoyama
Photography:
Hideo Kanno

R30 SWEET J-POPS
-JAZZ-

PROJECT

R30 Sweet J-Pop JAZZ,
CD package,
M&I Company Ltd.

COUNTRY

Japan

YEAR

2008

DESIGN

ALFAEYES design Inc.

TEAM

Yoshie Yokoyama

PROJECT
RABAN / Shinji Tanimura,
DVD package, Pony
Canyon Inc.

COUNTRY
Japan

YEAR
2002

DESIGN
ALFAEYES design Inc.

TEAM
Design:
Yoshie Yokoyama
Photography:
Kurou Doi

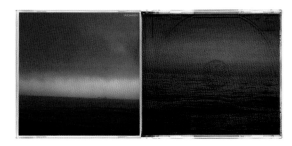

PROJECT
RADIO / Screaming Poets,
DVD package, Pony
Canyon Inc.

COUNTRY
Japan

YEAR
2000

DESIGN
ALFAEYES design Inc.

TEAM
Design:
Yoshie Yokoyama
Photography:
Kenji Kubo

project
Driving Bay Blues / Shima
Takada, *CD package*,
EMI Music Japan Inc.

country
Japan

year
2003

design
ALFAEYES design Inc.

team
Design:
Yoshie Yokoyama
Photography:
Akitada Hamasaki

PROJECT
Smooth Jazz -VOICE- /
V.A., *CD package*,
M&I Company Ltd.

COUNTRY
Japan

YEAR
2006

DESIGN
ALFAEYES design Inc.

TEAM
Design:
Yoshie Yokoyama
Illustration:
Kenta Ueoka

PROJECT

Innocent / Zoophilia,
CD package, Columbia
Music Entertainment Inc.

COUNTRY

Japan

YEAR

2002

DESIGN

ALFAEYES design Inc.

TEAM

Design:
Yoshie Yokoyama
Photography:
Jin Ohashi

project
Ha Tran 9803, *CD package*,
Ha Tran Productions

country
Vietnam

year
2004

design
Dzungyoko

team
Photography:
Tran Tien Dung

HA TRAN
9803

1. Mùa xuân gọi
   Trần Tiến
2. Mưa tháng Giêng
   Việt Hùng
3. Phố nghèo
   Trần Tiến
4. Lời chưa nói
   Xuân Phương
5. Tình ca
   Quốc Bảo
6. Hoa gạo
   Nhạc: Ngọc Đại, thơ: Phan Huyền Thư
7. Chuyện tình thảo nguyên
   Trần Tiến
8. Sắc màu
   Trần Tiến
9. Chạy trốn
   Lê Minh Sơn
10. Em về tóc xanh
    Quốc Bảo
11. Em về tình khôi
    Quốc Bảo
12. Dấu phố em qua
    Nguyễn Bình
13. Dòng sông mùa thu
    Trần Tiến

HA TRAN PRODUCTIONS

PROJECT
Communication 06,
CD package, Ha Tran
Productions

COUNTRY
Vietnam

YEAR
2008

DESIGN
Dzungyoko

TEAM
Photography:
Phan Hoai Nam

Love Songs 1, *CD package*,
Tung Duong Productions

Vietnam

2010

Dzungyoko

Photography:
Samuel Hoang

PROJECT

Earth Beat / Gocco+GoRo,
CD package, Edoya
Corporation

COUNTRY

Japan

YEAR

2008

DESIGN

Minato Ishikawa
Associates Inc.

TEAM

Art Direction/Art:
Minato Ishikawa
Design:
Kayoko Akiyama

project
Shinji Ra Munita / Shinji
Tanimura, *DVD package*,
Pony Canyon Inc.

country
Japan

year
2000

design
ALFAEYES design Inc.

team
Yoshie Yokoyama

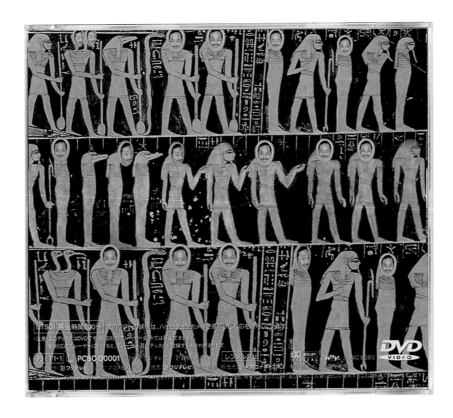

2 Cô Đơn - Đỗ Bảo

Ai gọi tôi lúc này, ngoài trời heo hắt cơn mưa mùa xuân.
Khi tôi phải đi, tôi phải đi.
Bỏ lại chiếc tách bên bàn chưa cất.
Bỏ lại ánh sáng trong phòng chưa tắt.
Bỏ lại những chiếc áo bộn bề dưới đất.
Bỏ lại những bức tường cô đơn, không quen ai, chỉ mỗi tôi.

Tôi gặp đêm đã khuya, gió khải cuộc hoang vu những mái hiên nhà.
Cây bàng xòe tóc xanh, những khi trời mưa, sương ướt long lanh.
U huyền những ngã tư, quán ai mở khuya khách gió khách mưa.
Như bộ phim trắng đen, vẫn câu chuyện đêm khuya, vẫn tôi.
Những ngõ sâu ẩm ướt lạnh lẽo. Bóng mưa loang bò theo len lén.
Uhh... Nỗi cô đơn cùng đêm cùng đệm.

Ở thẳm sâu mùa xuân màn sương bụi mưa về đâu sợi khói bé nhỏ.
Cả miền đất im lặng, cuộc sống im lặng chỉ gió thổi chỉ nước lăn dòng khơi.
Tôi như đêm, tôi như mưa, tôi như cây, tôi như những ngõ tối.
Lại thao thức an ủi những câu chuyện của đêm khuya.
Lại những bước đêm buồn sẽ bước đêm.
Đi từ cảnh cửa của đêm trắng, đi từ căn nhà đèn chưa tắt.

7 Đỉnh Núi Lãng Quên - Đỗ Bảo

Bao nhiêu nỗi nhớ, có buồn đêm vắng.
Biết anh có nghe nơi căn phòng nào.
Bao nhiêu đêm trắng, bầu trời râm ran.
Ngoài núi rừng xao xác bừng nở.
Những loài hoa mới, những dòng suối mới,
những cuộc vui mới chỉ em thâu đêm cô đơn căng đầy ngực tức
mong anh ,được say với anh.
Dịu ngọt một đời nếu là sống với anh, được ngủ một ngày nếu là chết với anh.
Được yêu như cứu anh, yêu như hình bóng anh.
Xa dòng sông ấy xa điệu nhạc ấy nơi mà em chưa đi tới.
Xa loài hoa ấy, xa ngọn núi ấy nơi mà em chưa bước tới

Làm sao anh biết lẻ đêm vắng anh,
anh đâu biết bầu trời rợn ngợp của hoang mang.
Anh đâu biết thảo nguyên gió lồng lộng thế nào.
Anh đâu biết nơi trăm bề gió hú, nơi u buồn rẽ nhánh mọc lên
rất nhanh cả thảo nguyên khao khát.

Nỗi khát lan đi loang đi mang em về bờ suối hoang vắng.
Nhức nhối lan đi loang đi rừng hoa vắng.
Nỗi buồn xanh bốn bề này mầm thảo nguyên âm rung chuông khánh.
Em chạy. Em cười. Em nhìn đỉnh núi lãng quên đang gọi mời.

Giữa phút giây cheo leo em bỗng lo sợ dòng suối u ám.
Giữa phút giây cheo leo em muốn trốn khỏi bóng tối.
Nỗi buồn không dừng cuộc này mầm tim em oằn dưới nhát búa.
Như đã ở đó lâu rồi. Anh ngồi cô đơn nhìn em đang tới.
Như đã ở đó lâu rồi. Anh ngồi cô đơn nhìn em đang tới.

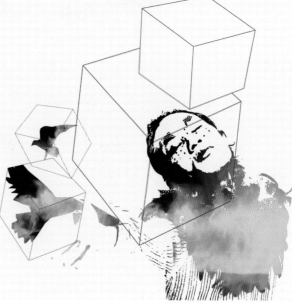

PROJECT
Colour of the cube,
CD package, Tung Duong
Productions

COUNTRY
Vietnam

YEAR
2008

DESIGN
Dzungyoko

TEAM
Photography:
Pham Hoai Nam

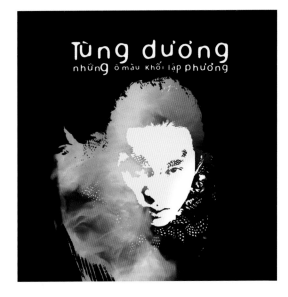

INDEX

acknowledgements

About five years ago we published a book exclusively on Japanese graphic design. It was a success, much more than we expected, and we felt it was now the right time to expand the range of our survey in the region. Living in Japan for three and a half years, I had the chance to travel quite a few times throughout Asia, and to discover how diverse the continent is. Diversity is for me the key ingredient that fuels creativity, and that is what this book is all about.

The extensive research it required was also a discovery process for me, and one I hope we can pass on to designers and creative professionals worldwide. To accomplish the research and produce this survey, I had with me two experts in Asian design, Bruno Porto, professor in Shanghai, and Sadao Maekawa, ex-colleague and today a PhD researcher into creativity and technology in Tokyo. Without them, and Daniel Siciliano Bretas, my constant right hand, project manager, editor, and designer of this publication, this book could never have been put together. Moreover, we were honoured to have the invaluable contribution of Min Wang, professor and design director for the Beijing 2008 Olympic Games, and Huang Li, Editor-in-chief of *Package & Design Magazine* of China.

I also have to thank the design studios, agencies, magazines, and branding agencies that submitted their incredible work, including those whose work was ultimately not included in the book. We look forward to working with all of you in the future! Thank you also to Jutta Hendricks, whose unstinting attention to detail has contributed immensely to the quality of this book and to others I have edited. Finally, thank you to Stefan Klatte in production, it has been a pleasure to work with him once again. The team in Germany has done an amazing job! I am sure that you will find many projects here to interest and inspire you. Happy reading!

Julius Wiedemann

© 2010 TASCHEN GmbH
Hohenzollernring 53, D-50672 Köln
www.taschen.com

To stay informed about upcoming TASCHEN titles, please
request our magazine at www.taschen.com/magazine or
write to TASCHEN, Hohenzollernring 53, D-50672 Cologne,
Germany, contact@taschen.com, Fax: +49 221 254919.
We will be happy to send you a free copy of our magazine
which is filled with information about all of our books.

Editor
Julius Wiedemann
Editorial Coordination
Daniel Siciliano Bretas
Collaboration
Jutta Hendricks

Design
Daniel Siciliano Bretas
Production
Stefan Klatte

English Revision
Chris Allen
French Translation
Valérie Lavoyer for Equipo de Edición
German Translation
Jürgen Dubau

Printed in Italy
ISBN 978–3–8365–1899–4